Workshop on Distributed Semantics and Compositionality 2011

(DiSCo 2011)

Held at ACL HLT 2011

Portland, Oregon, USA
24 June 2011

ISBN: 978-1-61839-250-3

Printed from e-media with permission by:

Curran Associates, Inc.
57 Morehouse Lane
Red Hook, NY 12571

Some format issues inherent in the e-media version may also appear in this print version.

Printed by Curran Associates, Inc. (2011)

For permission requests, please contact the Association for Computational Linguistics at the address below.

Association for Computational Linguistics
209 N. Eighth Street
Stroudsburg, Pennsylvania 18360

Phone: 1-570-476-8006
Fax: 1-570-476-0860

acl@aclweb.org

Additional copies of this publication are available from:

Curran Associates, Inc.
57 Morehouse Lane
Red Hook, NY 12571 USA
Phone: 845-758-0400
Fax: 845-758-2634
Email: curran@proceedings.com
Web: www.proceedings.com

Introduction

Any NLP system that does semantic processing relies on the assumption of semantic compositionality: the meaning of a phrase is determined by the meanings of its parts and their combination. For this, it is necessary to have automatic methods that are capable to reproduce the compositionality of language.

Recent years have shown the renaissance of interest in distributional semantics. While distributional methods in semantics have proven to be very efficient in tackling a wide range of tasks in natural language processing, e.g., document retrieval, clustering and classification, question answering, query expansion, word similarity, synonym extraction, relation extraction, and many others, they are still strongly limited by being inherently word-based. The main hurdle for vector space models to further progress is the ability to handle compositionality.

The workshop is of potential interest to the researchers working on distributional semantics and compositionality as well as for those interested in extracting non-compositional phrases from large corpora by applying distributional methods that assign a graded compositionality score to a phrase. This score denotes the extent to which the compositionality assumption holds for a given expression. The latter can be used, for example, to decide whether the phrase should be treated as a single unit in applications or included in a dictionary. We have emphasized that the focus is on automatically acquiring semantic compositionality, thereby explicitly avoiding approaches that employ prefabricated lists of non-compositional phrases.

This volume contains papers accepted for publication at DiSCo'2011 Workshop on Distributional Semantics and Compositionality, collocated with ACL-HLT 2011, the 49th Annual Meeting of the Association for Computational Linguistics: Human Language Technologies.

The workshop consists of a main session and a shared task. To the best of our knowledge, this has been the first attempt in the community to offer a dataset and a shared task that allows to explicitly evaluate the models of graded compositionality for phrases per se that occur in three types of grammatical relations: adjective-noun pairs, subject-verb and verb-object pairs in English and German.

For the main session, one long and two short papers have been accepted for publication. Further, seven teams with 19 systems have taken part in the shared task. We consider this a success, taking into consideration that the task is new and difficult.

The description of the task and the results of evaluation are part of these proceedings. In short, approaches ranging from pure statistical association measures to various variations of word space models have been applied to solve the DiSCo task. Six system description papers have been accepted for publication.

Both regular and system description papers have been carefully reviewed by the program committee. We would like to thank the committee for insightful and timely reviews (in spite of the Easter holidays).

The accepted regular articles address a rather wide spectrum of issues within distributional semantics, such as:

- automatic detection of semantic deviance in attributive Adjective-Noun (AN) expressions with four compositional methods for distributional vectors (Vecchi, Baroni and Zamparelli, 2011);

- encoding syntactic trees in distributed vectors and the application of those for recognizing textual entailment (RTE) (Zanzotto and Dell'Arciprete, 2011);
- two possible generalizations of pointwise mutual information for three-way distributional models (Van de Cruys, 2011).

Last but not least, we would like to thank Dominic Widdows for agreeing to give an invited talk about the theory and practice behind some of recent developments in semantic vectors.

Enjoy the workshop!

The organizers:

- Chris Biemann, UKP lab, TU Darmstadt, Germany
- Eugenie Giesbrecht, FZI Forschungszentrum Informatik[1] at the University of Karlsruhe, Germany

[1]Research Center for Information Technology

Organizers:

Chris Biemann, UKP lab, TU Darmstadt, Germany
Eugenie Giesbrecht, FZI Forschungszentrum Informatik, Karlsruhe, Germany

Program Committee:

Enrique Alfonseca, Google Research, Switzerland
Tim Baldwin, University of Melbourne, Australia
Marco Baroni, University of Trento, Italy
Paul Buitelaar, National University of Ireland, Ireland
Chris Brockett, Microsoft Research, Redmond, US
Tim van de Cruys, University of Cambridge, UK
Stefan Evert, University of Osnabrück, Germany
Antske Fokkens, Saarland University, Germany
Silvana Hartmann, TU Darmstadt, Germany
Alfio Massimiliano Gliozzo, IBM, Hawthorne, NY, USA
Mirella Lapata, University of Edinburgh, UK
Ted Pedersen, University of Minnesota, Duluth, USA
Yves Peirsman, Stanford University, USA
Sebastian Rudolph, Karlsruhe Institute of Technology, Germany
Peter D. Turney, National Research Council Canada, Canada
Magnus Sahlgren, Gavagai, Sweden
Serge Sharoff, University of Leeds, UK
Anders Søgaard, University of Copenhagen, Denmark
Daniel Sonntag, German Research Center for AI, Germany
Diana McCarthy, Lexical Computing Ltd., UK
Dominic Widdows, Google, USA

Invited Speaker:

Dominic Widdows, Google, USA

supported by

THESEUS

Google

FZI

Table of Contents

Conference Program

Friday June 24, 2011

9:20–9:30 Opening

09:30–10:30 Invited Talk by Dominic Widdows

10:30–11:00 Morning break

11:00–11:40 *(Linear) Maps of the Impossible: Capturing Semantic Anomalies in Distributional Space*
Eva Maria Vecchi, Marco Baroni and Roberto Zamparelli

11:40–12:05 *Distributed Structures and Distributional Meaning*
Fabio Massimo Zanzotto and Lorenzo Dell'Arciprete

12:05–12:30 *Two Multivariate Generalizations of Pointwise Mutual Information*
Tim Van de Cruys

12:30–14:00 Lunch break

14:00–14:30 *Distributional Semantics and Compositionality 2011: Shared Task Description and Results*
Chris Biemann and Eugenie Giesbrecht

14:30–14:50 *Shared Task System Description: Frustratingly Hard Compositionality Prediction*
Anders Johannsen, Hector Martinez, Christian Rishøj and Anders Søgaard

14:50–15:10 *Identifying Collocations to Measure Compositionality: Shared Task System Description*
Ted Pedersen

15:10–15:30 *Shared Task System Description: Measuring the Compositionality of Bigrams using Statistical Methodologies*
Tanmoy Chakraborty, Santanu Pal, Tapabrata Mondal, Tanik Saikh and Sivaju Bandyopadhyay

15:30–16:00 Afternoon break

16:00–16:20 *Detecting Compositionality Using Semantic Vector Space Models Based on Syntactic Context. Shared Task System Description*
Guillermo Garrido and Anselmo Peñas

Friday June 24, 2011 (continued)

(Linear) Maps of the Impossible: Capturing semantic anomalies in distributional space

Eva Maria Vecchi and **Marco Baroni** and **Roberto Zamparelli**
Center for Mind/Brain Sciences, University of Trento
Rovereto (TN), Italy
{evamaria.vecchi-1,marco.baroni,roberto.zamparelli}@unitn.it

Abstract

In this paper, we present a first attempt to characterize the semantic deviance of composite expressions in distributional semantics. Specifically, we look for properties of adjective-noun combinations within a vector-based semantic space that might cue their lack of meaning. We evaluate four different compositionality models shown to have various levels of success in representing the meaning of AN pairs: the simple additive and multiplicative models of Mitchell and Lapata (2008), and the linear-map-based models of Guevara (2010) and Baroni and Zamparelli (2010). For each model, we generate composite vectors for a set of AN combinations unattested in the source corpus and which have been deemed either *acceptable* or *semantically deviant*. We then compute measures that might cue semantic anomaly, and compare each model's results for the two classes of ANs. Our study shows that simple, unsupervised cues can indeed significantly tell unattested but acceptable ANs apart from impossible, or deviant, ANs, and that the simple additive and multiplicative models are the most effective in this task.

1 Introduction

Statistical approaches to describe, represent and understand natural language have been criticized as failing to account for linguistic 'creativity', a property which has been accredited to the compositional nature of natural language. Specifically, criticisms against statistical methods were based on the argument that a corpus cannot significantly sample a natural language because natural language is infinite (Chomsky, 1957). This cricticism also applies to distributional semantic models that build semantic representations of words or phrases in terms of vectors recording their distributional co-occurrence patterns in a corpus (Turney and Pantel, 2010), but have no obvious way to generalize to word combinations that have not been observed in the corpus. To address this problem, there have been several recent attempts to incorporate into distributional semantic models a component that generates vectors for unseen linguistic structures by compositional operations in the vector space (Baroni and Zamparelli, 2010; Guevara, 2010; Mitchell and Lapata, 2010).

The ability to work with unattested data leads to the question of why a linguistic expression might not be attested in even an extremely large and well-balanced corpus. Its absence might be motivated by a number of factors: pure chance, the fact that the expression is ungrammatical, uses a rare structure, describes false facts, or, finally, is *nonsensical*. One criticism from generative linguists is precisely that statistical methods could not distinguish between these various possibilities.

The difficulty of solving this problem can be illustrated by the difference in semantics between the adjective-noun pairs in (1a) and (1b):

(1) a. blue rose
b. residential steak

Although it may be the case that you have never ac-

Proceedings of the Workshop on Distributional Semantics and Compositionality (DiSCo'2011), pages 1–9,
Portland, Oregon, 24 June 2011.

tually seen a *blue rose*, the concept is not inconceivable. On the other hand, the concept of a *residential steak* is rather unimaginable, and intuitively its absence in a corpus is motivated by more than just chance or data sparseness.

The present paper is a first attempt to use compositionality and distributional measures to distinguish nonsensical, or semantically deviant, linguistic expression from other types of unattested structures. The task of distinguishing between unattested but **acceptable** and unattested but **semantically deviant** linguistic expressions is not only a way to address the criticism about the meaning of 'unattestedness', but also a task that could have a large impact on the (computational) linguistic community as a whole (see Section 2.1).

Our specific goal is to automatically detect semantic deviance in attributive Adjective-Noun (AN) expressions, using a small number of simple cues in the vectorial representation of an AN as it is generated from the distributional vectors of its component A and N by four compositional models found in the literature. The choice of AN as our testbed is motivated by two facts: first of all, ANs are common, small constituents containing no functional material, and secondly, ANs have already been studied in compositional distributional semantics (Baroni and Zamparelli, 2010; Guevara, 2010; Mitchell and Lapata, 2010).

It is important to note that in this research we talk about 'semantically deviant' expressions, but we do not exclude the possibility that such expressions are interpreted as metaphors, via a chain of associations. In fact, distributional measures are desirable models to account for this, since they naturally lead to a gradient notion of semantic anomaly.

The rest of this paper is structured as follows. Section 2 discusses relevant earlier work, introducing the literature on semantic deviance as well as compositional methods in distributional semantics. Section 3 presents some hypotheses about cues of semantic deviance in distributional space. Our experimental setup and procedure are detailed in Section 4, whereas the experiments' results are presented and analyzed in Section 5. We conclude by summarizing and proposing future directions in Section 6.

2 Related work

2.1 Semantic deviance

As far as we know, we are the first to try to model semantic deviance using distributional methods, but the issue of when a complex linguistic expression is semantically deviant has been addressed since the 1950's in various areas of linguistics. In computational linguistics, the possibility of detecting semantic deviance has been seen as a prerequisite to access metaphorical/non-literal semantic interpretations (Fass and Wilks, 1983; Zhou et al., 2007). In psycholinguistics, it has been part of a wide debate on the point at which context can make us perceive a 'literal' vs. a 'figurative' meaning (Giora, 2002). In theoretical generative linguistics, the issue was originally part of a discussion on the boundaries between syntax and semantics. Cases like Chomsky's classic "*Colorless green ideas sleep furiously*" can actually be regarded as violations of very fine-grained syntactic *selectional restrictions* on the arguments of verbs or modifiers, on the model of **much computer* (arguably a failure of *much* to combine with a noun +COUNT). By 1977, even Chomsky doubted that speakers could in general have intuitions about whether ill-formedness was syntactic or semantic (Chomsky, 1977, p. 4). The spirit of the selectional approach persists in Asher (2011), who proposes a detailed system of semantic types plus a theory of type coercion, designed to account for the shift in meaning seen in, e.g., (2) (*lunch* as food or as an event).

(2) Lunch was delicious but took forever.

A practical problem with this approach is that a full handmade specification of the features that determine semantic compatibility is a very expensive and time-consuming enterprise, and it should be done consistently across the whole content lexicon. Moreover, it is unclear how to model the intuition that *naval fraction*, *musical North* or *institutional acid* sound odd, in the absence of very particular contexts, while (2) sounds quite natural. Whatever the nature of coercion, we do not want it to run so smoothly that any combination of A and N (or V and its arguments) becomes meaningful and completely acceptable.

2.2 Distributional approaches to meaning composition

Although the issue of how to compose meaning has attracted interest since the early days of distributional semantics (Landauer and Dumais, 1997), recently a very general framework for modeling compositionality has been proposed by Mitchell and Lapata (Mitchell and Lapata, 2008; Mitchell and Lapata, 2009; Mitchell and Lapata, 2010). Given two vectors $\mathbf{u}$ and $\mathbf{v}$, they identify two general classes of composition models, (linear) additive models:

$$\mathbf{p} = \mathbf{A}\mathbf{u} + \mathbf{B}\mathbf{v} \quad (1)$$

where $\mathbf{A}$ and $\mathbf{B}$ are weight matrices, and multiplicative models:

$$\mathbf{p} = \mathbf{C}\mathbf{u}\mathbf{v}$$

where $\mathbf{C}$ is a weight tensor projecting the $\mathbf{u}\mathbf{v}$ tensor product onto the space of $\mathbf{p}$. Mitchell and Lapata derive two simplified models from these general forms: The simplified additive model given by $\mathbf{p} = \alpha\mathbf{u} + \beta\mathbf{v}$, and a simplified multiplicative approach that reduces to component-wise multiplication, where the i-th component of the composed vector is given by: $p_i = u_i v_i$. Mitchell and Lapata evaluate the simplified models on a wide range of tasks ranging from paraphrasing to statistical language modeling to predicting similarity intuitions. Both simple models fare quite well across tasks and alternative semantic representations, also when compared to more complex methods derived from the equations above. Given their overall simplicity, good performance and the fact that they have also been extensively tested in other studies (Baroni and Zamparelli, 2010; Erk and Padó, 2008; Guevara, 2010; Kintsch, 2001; Landauer and Dumais, 1997), we re-implement here both the simplified additive and simplified multiplicative methods (we do not, however, attempt to tune the weights of the additive model, although we do apply a scalar normalization constant to the adjective and noun vectors).

Mitchell and Lapata (as well as earlier researchers) do not exploit corpus evidence about the $\mathbf{p}$ vectors that result from composition, despite the fact that it is straightforward (at least for short constructions) to extract direct distributional evidence about the composite items from the corpus (just collect co-occurrence information for the composite item from windows around the contexts in which it occurs). The main innovation of Guevara (2010), who focuses on adjective-noun combinations (AN), is to use the co-occurrence vectors of corpus-observed ANs to train a supervised composition model. Guevara, whose approach we also re-implement here, adopts the full additive composition form from Equation (1) and he estimates the $\mathbf{A}$ and $\mathbf{B}$ weights (concatenated into a single matrix, that acts as a linear map from the space of concatenated adjective and noun vectors onto the AN vector space) using partial least squares regression. The training data are pairs of adjective-noun vector concatenations, as input, and corpus-derived AN vectors, as output. Guevara compares his model to the simplified additive and multiplicative models of Mitchell and Lapata. Corpus-observed ANs are nearer, in the space of observed and predicted test set ANs, to the ANs generated by his model than to those from the alternative approaches. The additive model, on the other hand, is best in terms of shared neighbor count between observed and predicted ANs.

The final approach we re-implement is the one proposed by Baroni and Zamparelli (2010), who treat attributive adjectives as functions from noun meanings to noun meanings. This is a standard approach in Montague semantics (Thomason, 1974), except noun meanings here are distributional vectors, not denotations, and adjectives are (linear) functions learned from a large corpus. Unlike in Guevara's approach, a separate matrix is generated for each adjective using only examples of ANs containing that adjective, and no adjective vector is used: the adjective is represented entirely by the matrix mapping nouns to ANs. In terms of Mitchell and Lapata's general framework, this approach derives from the additive form in Equation (1) with the matrix multiplying the adjective vector (say, $\mathbf{A}$) set to $\mathbf{0}$, the other matrix ($\mathbf{B}$) representing the adjective at hand, and $\mathbf{v}$ a noun vector. Baroni and Zamparelli (2010) show that their model significantly outperforms other vector composition methods, including addition, multiplication and Guevara's approach, in the task of approximating the correct vectors for previously unseen (but corpus-attested) ANs. Simple addition emerges as the second best model.

See Section 4.3 below for details on our re-implementations. Note that they follow very closely the procedure of Baroni and Zamparelli (2010), including choices of source corpus and parameter values, so that we expect their results on the quality of the various models in predicting ANs to also hold for our re-implementations.

3 Simple indices of semantic deviance

We consider here a few simple, unsupervised measures to help us distinguish the representation that a distributional composition model generates for a semantically anomalous AN from the one it generates for a semantically acceptable AN. In both cases, we assume that the AN is not already part of the model semantic space, just like you can distinguish between *parliamentary tomato* (odd) and *marble iPad* (OK), although you probably never heard either expression.

We hypothesize that, since the values in the dimensions of a semantic space are a distributional proxy to the meaning of an expression, a meaningless expression should in general have low values across the semantic space dimensions. For example, a *parliamentary tomato*, no longer being a vegetable but being an unlikely parliamentary event, might have low values on both dimensions characterizing vegetables and dimensions characterizing events. Thus, our first simple measure of semantic anomaly is the **length** of the model-generated AN. We hypothesize that anomalous AN vectors are shorter than acceptable ANs.

Second, if deviant composition destroys or randomizes the meaning of a noun, as a side effect we might expect the resulting AN to be more distant, in the semantic space, from the component noun. Although even a *marble iPad* might have lost some essential properties of iPads (it could for example be an iPad statue you cannot use as a tablet), to the extent that we can make sense of it, it must retain at least some characteristics of iPads (at the very least, it will be shaped like an iPad). On the other hand, we cannot imagine what a *parliamentary tomato* should be, and thus cannot attribute even a subset of the regular tomato properties to it. We thus hypothesize that model-generated vectors of deviant ANs will form a wider angle (equivalently, will have a lower **cosine**) with the corresponding N vectors than acceptable ANs.

Finally, if an AN makes no sense, its model-generated vector should not have many neighbours in the semantic space, since our semantic space is populated by nouns, adjectives and ANs that are commonly encountered in the corpus, and should thus be meaningful. We expect deviant ANs to be "semantically isolated", a notion that we operationalize in terms of a (neighborhood) **density** measure, namely the average cosine with the (top 10) nearest neighbours. We hypothesize that model-generated vectors of deviant ANs will have lower density than model-generated acceptable ANs.

4 Experimental setup

4.1 Semantic space

Our initial step was to construct a semantic space for our experiments, consisting of a matrix where each row vector represents an adjective, noun or AN. We first introduce the source corpus, then the vocabulary of words and ANs that we represent in the space, and finally the procedure adopted to build the vectors representing the vocabulary items from corpus statistics, in order to obtain the semantic space matrix. We work here with a "vanilla" semantic space (essentially, we follow the steps of Baroni and Zamparelli (2010)), since our focus is on the effect of different composition methods given a common semantic space. We leave it to further work to study how choices in semantic space construction affect composition operations.

4.1.1 Source corpus

We use as our source corpus the concatenation of the Web-derived ukWaC corpus (`http://wacky.sslmit.unibo.it/`), a mid-2009 dump of the English Wikipedia (`http://en.wikipedia.org`) and the British National Corpus (`http://www.natcorp.ox.ac.uk/`). The corpus has been tokenized, POS-tagged and lemmatized with the TreeTagger (Schmid, 1995), and it contains about 2.8 billion tokens. We extract all statistics at the lemma level, ignoring inflectional information.

4.1.2 Semantic space vocabulary

The words/ANs in the semantic space must of course include the items that we need for our experiments (adjectives, nouns and ANs used for model training and as input to composition). Moreover, in order to study the behaviour of the test items we are interested in (that is, model-generated AN vectors) within a large and less ad-hoc space, we also include many more adjectives, nouns and ANs in our vocabulary not directly relevant to our experimental manipulations.

We populate our semantic space with the 8K most frequent nouns and 4K most frequent adjectives from the corpus (excluding, in both cases, the top 50 most frequent elements). We extended this vocabulary to include two sets of ANs (33K ANs cumulatively), for a total of 45K vocabulary items in the semantic space.

To create the ANs needed to run and evaluate the experiments described below, we focused on a set of adjectives which are very frequent in the corpus so that they will be in general able to combine with wide classes of nouns, making the unattested cases more interesting, but not so frequent as to have such a general meaning that would permit a free combination with nearly any noun. The ANs were therefore generated by crossing a selected set of 200 very frequent adjectives (adjectives attested in the corpus at least 47K times, and at most 740K) and the set of the 8K nouns in our semantic space vocabulary, producing a set of 4.92M generated ANs.

The first set of ANs included in the semantic space vocabulary is a randomly sampled set of 30K ANs from the generated set which are attested in the corpus at least 200 times (to avoid noise and focus on ANs for which we can extract reasonably robust distributional data). We also extracted any unattested ANs from the set of generated set (about 3.5M unattested ANs), putting them aside to later assemble our evaluation material, described in Section 4.2.

To add further variety to the semantic space, we included a less controlled second set of 3K ANs randomly picked among those that are attested and are formed by the combination of any of the 4K adjectives and 8K nouns in the vocabulary.

4.1.3 Semantic space construction

For each of the items in our vocabulary, we first build 10K-dimensional vectors by recording their sentence-internal co-occurrence with the top 10K most frequent content words (nouns, adjectives or verbs) in the corpus. The raw co-occurrence counts are then transformed into Local Mutual Information scores (Local Mutual Information is an association measure that closely approximates the commonly used Log-Likelihood Ratio while being simpler to compute (Baroni and Lenci, 2010; Evert, 2005)).

Next, we reduce the full co-occurrence matrix applying the Singular Value Decomposition (SVD) operation, like in LSA and related distributional semantic methods (Landauer and Dumais, 1997; Rapp, 2003; Schütze, 1997). The original 45K-by-10K-dimensional matrix is reduced in this way to a 45K-by-300 matrix, where vocabulary items are represented by their coordinates in the space spanned by the first 300 right singular vectors of the SVD solution. This step is motivated by the fact that we will estimate linear models to predict the values of each dimension of an AN from the dimensions of the components. We thus prefer to work in a smaller and denser space. As a sanity check, we verify that we obtain state-of-the-art-range results on various semantic tasks using this reduced semantic space (not reported here for space reason).

4.2 Evaluation materials

Our goal is to study what happens when compositional methods are used to construct a distributional representation for ANs that are semantically deviant, compared to the AN representations they generate for ANs they have not encountered before, but that are semantically acceptable.

In order to assemble these lists, we started from the set of 3.5M unattested ANs described in Section 4.1.2 above, focusing on 30 randomly chosen adjectives. For each of these, we randomly picked 100 ANs for manual inspection (3K ANs in total). Two authors went through this list, marking those ANs that they found semantically highly anomalous, no matter how much effort one would put in constructing metaphorical or context-dependent interpretations, as well as those they found completely acceptable (so, rating was on a 3-way scale: deviant, intermediate, acceptable). The rating exercise resulted in rather low agreement (Cohen's $\kappa = 0.32$), but we reasoned that those relatively few cases (456 over 3K) where both judges agreed the AN was odd should indeed be odd, and similarly for the even rarer cases in which they agreed an AN was completely acceptable (334 over 3K). We thus used the agreed deviant and acceptable ANs as test data.

Of 30 adjectives, 5 were discarded for either technical reasons or for having less than 5 agreed deviant or acceptable ANs. This left us with a **deviant AN test set** comprising of 413 ANs, on average 16 for each of the 25 remaining adjectives. Some examples of ANs in this set are: *academic bladder*, *blind pronunciation*, *parliamentary potato* and *sharp glue*. The **acceptable** (but unattested) **AN test set** contains 280 ANs, on average 11 for each of the 25 studied adjectives. Examples of ANs in this set include: *vulnerable gunman*, *huge joystick*, *academic crusade* and *blind cook*. The evaluation sets can be downloaded from `http://www.vecchi.com/eva/resources.html`.

There is no significant difference between the length of the vectors of the component nouns in the acceptable vs. deviant AN sets (two-tailed Welch's t test; $t = -0.25$; $p > 0.8$). This is important, since at least one of the potential cues to deviance we consider (AN vector length) is length-dependent, and we do not want a trivial result that can simply be explained by systematic differences in the length of the input vectors.

4.3 Composition methods

As discussed in Section 2.2, the experiment was carried out across four compositional methods.

Additive AN vectors (*add* method) are simply obtained by summing the corresponding adjective and noun vectors after normalizing them. **Multiplicative** vectors (*mult* method) were obtained by component-wise multiplication of the adjective and noun vectors, also after normalization. Confirming the results of Baroni and Zamparelli (2010), non-normalized versions of *add* and *mult* were also tested, but did not produce significant results (in the case of multiplication, normalization amounts to multiplying the composite vector by a scalar, so it only affects the length-dependent vector length measure). It is important to note that, as reported in Baroni and Zamparelli (2010), the *mult* method can be expected to perform better in the original, non-reduced semantic space because the SVD dimensions can have negative values, leading to counter-intuitive results with component-wise multiplication (multiplying large opposite-sign values results in large negative values instead of being cancelled out). The tests of Section 5, however, are each run in the SVD-reduced space to remain consistent across all models. We leave it to future work to explore the effect on the performance of using the non-reduced space for the models for which this option is computationally viable.

In the **linear map** (*lm*) approach proposed by Guevara (2010), a composite AN vector is obtained by multiplying a weight matrix by the concatenation of the adjective and noun vectors, so that each dimension of the generated AN vector is a linear combination of dimensions of the corresponding adjective and noun vectors. That is, the 600 weights in each of the 300 rows of the weight matrix are the coefficients of a linear equation predicting the values of a single dimension in the AN vector as a linear combination (weighted sum) of the 300 adjective and 300 noun dimensions. Following Guevara, we estimate the coefficients of the equation using (multivariate) partial least squares regression (PLSR) as implemented in the R `pls` package (Mevik and Wehrens, 2007), with the latent dimension parameter of PLSR set to 50, the same value used by Baroni and Zamparelli (2010). Coefficient matrix estimation is performed by feeding the PLSR a set of input-output examples, where the input is given by concatenated adjective and noun vectors, and the output is the vector of the corresponding AN directly extracted from our semantic space (i.e., the AN vectors used in training are not model-generated, but directly derived from corpus evidence about their distribution). The matrix is estimated using a random sample of 2K adjective-noun-AN tuples where the AN belongs to the set of 30K frequently attested ANs in our vocabulary.

Finally, in the **adjective-specific linear map** (*alm*) method of Baroni and Zamparelli (2010), an AN is generated by multiplying an adjective weight matrix with a noun vector. The weights of each of the 300 rows of the weight matrix are the coefficients of a linear equation predicting the values of one of the dimensions of the AN vector as a linear combination of the 300 dimensions of the component noun. The linear equation coefficients are estimated separately for each of the 25 tested adjectives from the attested noun-AN pairs containing that adjective (observed adjective vectors are not used), again using PLSR with the same parameter as above. For each adjective, the training N-AN vector pairs chosen are those available in the semantic space for each test set adjective, and range from 100 to more than 500 items across the 25 adjectives.

4.4 Experimental procedure

Using each composition method, we generate composite vectors for all the ANs in the two (acceptable and deviant) evaluation sets (see Section 4.2 above). We then compute the measures that might cue semantic deviance discussed in Section 3 above, and compare their values between the two AN sets. In order to smooth out adjective-specific effects, we z-normalize the values of each measure across all the ANs sharing an adjective before computing global statistics (i.e., the values for all ANs sharing an adjective from the two sets are transformed by subtracting their mean and dividing by their variance). We then compare the two sets, for each composition method and deviance cue, by means of two-tailed Welch's t tests. We report the estimated t score, that is, the standardized difference between the mean acceptable and deviant AN values, with the corresponding significance level. For all our cues, we predict t to be significantly larger than 0: Acceptable AN vectors should be *longer* than deviant ones, they should be *nearer* – that is, have a higher cosine with – the component N vectors and their neighbourhood should be *denser* – that is, the average cosines with their top neighbours should be higher than the ones of deviant ANs with their top neighbours.

5 Results

The results of our experiments are summarized in Table 1. We see that *add* and *mult* provide significant results in the expected direction for 2 over 3 cues, only failing the cosine test. With the *lm* model, acceptable and deviant ANs are indistinguishable across the board, whereas *alm* captures the distinction in terms of density.

	LENGTH		COSINE		DENSITY	
method	t	*sig.*	t	*sig.*	t	*sig.*
add	7.89	*	0.31		2.63	*
mult	3.16	*	-0.56		2.68	*
lm	0.16		0.55		-0.23	
alm	0.48		1.37		3.12	*

Table 1: t scores for difference between acceptable and deviant ANs with respect to 3 cues of deviance: *length* of the AN vector, *cosine* of the AN vector with the component noun vector and *density*, measured as the average cosine of an AN vector with its nearest 10 neighbours in semantic space. For all significant results, $p< 0.01$.

The high scores in the vector length analyses of both the addition and the multiplication models are an indication that semantically acceptable ANs tend to be composed of *similar* adjectives and nouns, i.e., those which occur in similar contexts and we can assume are likely to belong to the same domain, which sounds plausible.

In Baroni and Zamparelli (2010), the *alm* model performed far better than *add* and *mult* in approximating the correct vectors for unseen ANs, while on this (in a sense, more metalinguistic) task *add* and *mult* work better, while *alm* is successful only in the more sophisticated measure of neighbor density.

The lack of significant results for the cosine measure is disappointing, but not entirely surprising. A large angle between N and AN might be a feature of impossible ANs common to various types of possible ANs: idioms (a *red herring* is probably far from *herring* in semantic space), non-subsective adjectives (*stone lion* vs. *lion*; *fake butterfly* vs. *butterfly*), plus some metaphorical constructions (*academic crusade* vs. *crusade*—one of several ANs judged acceptable in our study, which can only be taken as metaphors). Recall, finally, that the vector for the base N collapses together all the meanings of an ambiguous N. The adjective might have a disambiguating effect which would increase the cosine distance.

To gain a better understanding of the neighborhood density test we performed a detailed analysis of the nearest neighbors of the AN vectors generated by the three models in which the difference in neighbor distance was significant across deviant and acceptable ANs: *alm*, multiplication and addition. For each of the ANs, we looked at the top 10 semantic-space neighbors generated by each of the three models, focusing on two aspects: whether the neighbor was a single A or N, rather than AN, and whether the neighbor contained the same A or N as the AN is was the neighbor of (as in *blind regatta / blind athlete* or *biological derivative / partial derivative*). The results are summarized in Table 2.

method	*status*	A *only*	N *only*	$A_1 = A_2$	$N_1 = N_2$
add	accept	11.9	8.7	14.6	2.4
	deviant	12.5	6.8	14.6	2.3
mult	accept	6.9	8.0	0.7	0.1
	deviant	2.7	7.3	0.5	0.1
alm	accept	4.9	17.7	7.0	0.0
	deviant	7.1	19.6	6.2	0.0

Table 2: Percentage distributions of various properties of the top 10 neighbours of ANs in the acceptable (2800) and deviant (4130) sets for *add*, *mult* and *alm*. The last two columns express whether the neighbor contains the same Adjective or Noun as the target AN.

In terms of the properties we measured, neighbor distributions are quite similar across acceptable and deviant ANs. One interesting finding is that the system is quite 'adjective-driven': particularly for the additive model (where we can imagine that some Ns with low dimensional values do not shift much the adjective position in the multidimensional space), less so in the *alm* method, and not at all for *mult*. To put the third and forth columns in context, the subset of the semantic space used to generate the SVD from which the neighbors are drawn contained 2.69% adjectives, 5.24% nouns and 92.07% ANs. With respect to the last two columns, it is interesting to observe that matching As are frequent for deviant ANs even in *alm*, a model which has never seen A-vectors during training. Further qualitative evaluations show that in many deviant AN cases the similarity is between the A in the target AN and the N of the neighbor (e.g. *academic bladder / honorary lectureship*), while the opposite effect seems to be much harder to find.

6 Conclusion and future work

The main aim of this paper was to propose a new challenge to the computational distributional semantics community, namely that of characterizing what happens, distributionally, when composition leads to semantically anomalous composite expressions. The hope is, on the one hand, to bring further support to the distributional approach by showing that it can be both productive and constrained; and on the other, to provide a more general characterization of the somewhat elusive notion of semantic deviance – a notion that the field of formal semantics acknowledges but might lack the right tools to model.

Our results are very preliminary, but also very encouraging, suggesting that simple unsupervised cues can significantly tell unattested but acceptable ANs apart from impossible, or at least deviant, ones. Although, somewhat disappointingly, the model that has been shown in a previous study (Baroni and Zamparelli, 2010) to be the best at capturing the semantics of well-formed ANs turns out to be worse than simple addition and multiplication.

Future avenues of research must include, first of all, an exploration on the effect on each model when tested in the non-reduced space where computationally possible, or using different dimensionality reduction methods. A preliminary study demonstrates an enhanced performance of the *mult* method in the full space.

Second, we hope to provide a larger benchmark of acceptable and deviant ANs, beyond the few hundreds we used here, and sampling a larger typology of ANs across frequency ranges and adjective and noun classes. To this extent, we are implementing a crowd-sourcing study to collect human judgments from a large pool of speakers on a much larger set of ANs unattested in the corpus. Averaging over multiple judgments, we will also be able to characterize semantic deviance as a gradient property, probably more accurately.

Next, the range of cues we used was quite limited, and we intend to extend the range to include more sophisticated methods such as 1) combining multiple cues in a single score; 2) training a supervised classifier from labeled acceptable and deviant ANs, and studying the most distinctive features discovered by the classifier; 3) trying more complex unsupervised techniques, such as using graph-theoretical methods to characterize the semantic neighborhood of ANs beyond our simple density measure.

Finally, we are currently not attempting a typology of deviant ANs. We do not distinguish cases such as *parliamentary tomato*, where the adjective does not apply to the conceptual semantic type of the noun (or at least, where it is completely undetermined which relation could bridge the two objects), from oxymorons such as *dry water*, or vacuously redundant ANs (*liquid water*) and so on. We realize that, at a more advanced stage of the analysis, some of these categories might need to be explicitly distinguished (for example, *liquid water* is odd but perfectly meaningful), leading to a multi-way task. Similarly, among acceptable ANs, there are special classes of expressions, such as idiomatic constructions, metaphors or other rhetorical figures, that might be particularly difficult to distinguish from deviant ANs. Again, more cogent tasks involving such well-formed but non-literal constructions (beyond the examples that ended up by chance in our acceptable set) are left to future work.

Acknowledgments

We thank Raffaella Bernardi, Gemma Boleda, Louise McNally and the anonymous reviewers for their advice and comments.

References

Nicholas Asher. 2011. *Lexical Meaning in Context: A Web of Words*. Cambridge University Press.

Marco Baroni and Alessandro Lenci. 2010. Distributional Memory: A general framework for corpus-based semantics. *Computational Linguistics*, 36(4):673–721.

Marco Baroni and Roberto Zamparelli. 2010. Nouns are vectors, adjectives are matrices: Representing adjective-noun constructions in semantic space. In *Proceedings of EMNLP*, pages 1183–1193, Boston, MA.

Noam Chomsky. 1957. *Syntactic Structures*. Mouton.

Noam Chomsky. 1977. *Essays on Form and Interpretation*. North Holland, New York.

Katrin Erk and Sebastian Padó. 2008. A structured vector space model for word meaning in context. In *Proceedings of EMNLP*, pages 897–906, Honolulu, HI, USA.

Stefan Evert. 2005. *The Statistics of Word Cooccurrences*. Dissertation, Stuttgart University.

Dan Fass and Yorick Wilks. 1983. Preference semantics, ill-formedness, and metaphor. *Computational Linguistics*, 9:178–187.

Rachel Giora. 2002. Literal vs. figurative language: Different or equal? *Journal of Pragmatics*, 34:487–506.

Emiliano Guevara. 2010. A regression model of adjective-noun compositionality in distributional semantics. In *Proceedings of the ACL GEMS Workshop*, pages 33–37, Uppsala, Sweden.

Walter Kintsch. 2001. Predication. *Cognitive Science*, 25(2):173–202.

Thomas Landauer and Susan Dumais. 1997. A solution to Plato's problem: The latent semantic analysis theory of acquisition, induction, and representation of knowledge. *Psychological Review*, 104(2):211–240.

Björn-Helge Mevik and Ron Wehrens. 2007. The pls package: Principal component and partial least squares regression in R. *Journal of Statistical Software*, 18(2). Published online: `http://www.jstatsoft.org/v18/i02/`.

Jeff Mitchell and Mirella Lapata. 2008. Vector-based models of semantic composition. In *Proceedings of ACL*, pages 236–244, Columbus, OH, USA.

Jeff Mitchell and Mirella Lapata. 2009. Language models based on semantic composition. In *Proceedings of EMNLP*, pages 430–439, Singapore.

Jeff Mitchell and Mirella Lapata. 2010. Composition in distributional models of semantics. *Cognitive Science*.

Reinhard Rapp. 2003. Word sense discovery based on sense descriptor dissimilarity. In *Proceedings of the 9th MT Summit*, pages 315–322, New Orleans, LA, USA.

Helmut Schmid. 1995. Improvements in part-of-speech tagging with an application to German. In *Proceedings of the EACL-SIGDAT Workshop*, Dublin, Ireland.

Hinrich Schütze. 1997. *Ambiguity Resolution in Natural Language Learning*. CSLI, Stanford, CA.

Richmond H Thomason, editor. 1974. *Formal Philosophy: Selected Papers of Richard Montague*. Yale University Press, New York.

Peter Turney and Patrick Pantel. 2010. From frequency to meaning: Vector space models of semantics. *Journal of Artificial Intelligence Research*, 37:141–188.

Chang-Le Zhou, Yun Yang, and Xiao-Xi Huang. 2007. Computational mechanisms for metaphor in languages: a survey. *Journal of Computer Science and Technology*, 22:308–319.

Distributed Structures and Distributional Meaning

Fabio Massimo Zanzotto
DISP University of Rome "Tor Vergata"
Via del Politecnico 1
00133 Roma, Italy
zanzotto@info.uniroma2.it

Lorenzo Dell'Arciprete
University of Rome "Tor Vergata"
Via del Politecnico 1
00133 Roma, Italy
lorenzo.dellarciprete@gmail.com

Abstract

Stemming from distributed representation theories, we investigate the interaction between distributed structure and distributional meaning. We propose a pure distributed tree (DT) and distributional distributed tree (DDT). DTs and DDTs are exploited for defining distributed tree kernels (DTKs) and distributional distributed tree kernels (DDTKs). We compare DTKs and DDTKs in two tasks: approximating tree kernels TK (Collins and Duffy, 2002); performing textual entailment recognition (RTE). Results show that DTKs correlate with TKs and perform in RTE better than DDTKs. Then, including distributional vectors in distributed structures is a very difficult task.

1 Introduction

Demonstrating that distributional semantics is a semantic model of natural language is a real research challenge in natural language processing. Frege's principle of compositionality (Frege, 1884), naturally taken into account in logic-based semantic models of natural language (Montague, 1974), is hardly effectively included in distributional semantics models. These models should compositionally derive distributional vectors for sentences and phrases from the distributional vectors of the composing words.

Besides vector averaging (Landauer and Dumais, 1997; Foltz et al., 1998), that can model distributional meaning of sentences, recent distributional compositional models focus on finding distributional vectors of word pairs (Mitchell and Lapata, 2010; Guevara, 2010; Baroni and Zamparelli, 2010; Zanzotto et al., 2010). Scaling up these 2-word sequence models to the sentence level is not trivial as syntactic structure of sentences plays a very important role. Understanding the relation between the structure and the meaning is needed for building distributional compositional models for sentences.

Research in Distributed Representations (DR) (Hinton et al., 1986) proposed models and methods for encoding data structures in vectors, matrices, or high-order tensors. Distributed Representations are oriented to preserve the structural information in the final representation. For this purpose, DR models generally use random and possibly orthogonal vectors for words and structural elements (Plate, 1994). As distributional semantics vectors are unlikely to be orthogonal, syntactic structure of sentences may be easily lost in the final vector combination.

In this paper, we investigate the interaction between distributed structure and distributional meaning by proposing a model to encode syntactic trees in distributed structures and by exploiting this model in kernel machines (Vapnik, 1995) to determine the similarity between syntactic trees. We propose a pure distributed tree (DT) and a distributional distributed tree (DDT). In line with the distributed representation theory, DTs use random vectors for representing words whereas DDTs use distributional vectors for words. Our interest is in understanding if the introduction of distributional semantic information in an inherently syntactic based model, such as distributed representations, leads to better performances in semantic aware tasks. DTs and DDTs are exploited for defining distributed tree ker-

Proceedings of the Workshop on Distributional Semantics and Compositionality (DiSCo'2011), pages 10–15,
Portland, Oregon, 24 June 2011.

nels (DTKs) and distributional distributed tree kernels (DDTKs). We study the interaction between structure and meaning in two ways: 1) by comparing DTKs and DDTKs with the classical tree similarity functions, i.e., the tree kernels TK (Collins and Duffy, 2002); 2) by comparing the accuracy of DTKs and DDTKs in a semantic task such as recognizing textual entailment (RTE). Results show that DTKs correlate with TKs and perform in RTE better than DDTKs. This indicates that including distributional vectors in distributed structures should be performed in a more complex fashion.

2 Related Work

Distributed Representations (DR) (Hinton et al., 1986) are models and methods for encoding data structures as trees in vectors, matrices, or high-order tensors. DR are studied in opposition to symbolic representations to describe how knowledge is treated in connectionist models (Rumelhart and Mcclelland, 1986). Basic symbolic elements, e.g., *John* or *car*, as well as eventually nested structures, e.g., *buy(John,car,in(1978))*, are represented as vectors, matrices, or higher order tensors. Vectors of basic elements (words, or concepts) can be randomly generated (e.g. (Anderson, 1973; Murdock, 1983)) or, instead, they may represent their attributes and can be manually built (e.g. (McRae et al., 1997; Andrews et al., 2009)). Vectors, matrices, or tensors for structures are compositionally derived using vectors for basic elements.

Good compositionally obtained vectors for structures are *explicit and immediately accessible*: information stored in a distributed representation should be easily accessible with simple operations (Plate, 1994). Circular convolution in Holographic Reduced Representations (HRRs) (Plate, 1994) is designed to satisfy the immediate accessibility property. It supports two operations for producing and accessing the compact representations: the circular convolution and the correlation. Given that component vectors are obtained randomly (as in (Anderson, 1973; Murdock, 1983)), correlation is the inverse of composition. Yet, distributed representations offer an informative way of encoding structures if basic vectors are nearly orthogonal.

3 Distributed Trees and Distributional Distributed Trees

Stemming from distributed representations, we propose a way to encode syntactic trees in distributed vectors. These vectors can be pure distributed tree vectors (DT) or distributional distributed tree vectors (DDT). Once defined, these vectors can be used as a tree similarity function in kernel machines (Vapnik, 1995). We can build pure distributed tree kernels (DTK) or distributional distributed tree kernels (DDTK) to be used in recognizing textual entailment (RTE).

The rest of the section is organized as follows. We firstly present the distributed trees and the distributed tree kernels (Sec. 3.1). We then describe how to obtain DTs and DDTs (Sec. 3.2). Finally, we describe how the related kernels can be used for the recognizing textual entailment task (Sec. 3.2.1).

3.1 Distributed Trees and Distributed Tree Kernels

We define a distributed vector in order to finally produce a similarity function between trees (i.e., a kernel function) as the classical tree kernel (Collins and Duffy, 2002). A distributed vector $\vec{\vec{T}}$ is a vector representing the subtrees of a tree T. The final function is:

$$\vec{\vec{T}} = \sum_{n \in N(T)} s(n) \qquad (1)$$

where $N(T)$ is the set of nodes of the tree T, n is a node, and $s(n)$ is the sum of the distributed vectors of the subtrees of T rooted in the node n. The function $s(n)$ is recursively defined as follows:

- $s(n) = \vec{n} \otimes \vec{w}$ if n is a pre-terminal node $n \rightarrow w$ where $\vec{n}$ is the vector representing n and $\vec{w}$ is the one representing the word w.

- $s(n) = \vec{n} \otimes (\vec{c_1} + s(c_1)) \otimes \ldots \otimes (\vec{c_n} + s(c_n))$ where n is not a pre-terminal node, $n \rightarrow c_1 \ldots c_n$ is the first production of the tree rooted in n, $\vec{n}$ is the vector of the node n, and $\vec{c_i}$ are the vectors of the nodes c_i.

The distributed vectors of the nodes only depend on tags of the nodes.

The function $\otimes$ is defined as the reverse element-wise product $\vec{v} = \vec{a} \otimes \vec{b}$ as:

$$v_i = \gamma a_i b_{n-i+1} \quad (2)$$

where v_i, a_i, and b_i are the elements of, respectively, the vectors $\vec{v}$, $\vec{a}$, and $\vec{b}$; n is the dimension of the space; and γ is a value to ensure that the operation $\otimes$ approximate the property of vector module preservation. This function is not commutative and this guarantees that different trees t have different vectors $\vec{t}$. It is possible to demonstrate that:

$$\vec{\tilde{T}} = \sum_{t \in S(T)} \vec{t} \quad (3)$$

where $S(T)$ is the set of the subtrees of T, t is one of its subtrees, and $\vec{t}$ is its distributed representation.

The distributed kernel $\widetilde{TK}$ function over trees then easily follows as:

$$\widetilde{TK}(T_1, T_2) = \vec{\tilde{T_1}} \cdot \vec{\tilde{T_2}} = \sum_{t_1 \in S(T_1)} \sum_{t_2 \in S(T_2)} \vec{t_1} \cdot \vec{t_2} \quad (4)$$

If the different trees are orthogonal, $\widetilde{TK}(T_1, T_2)$ counts approximately the number of subtrees in common between the two trees T_1 and T_2.

3.2 Pure Distributed vs. Distributional Distributed Trees

For producing the distributed trees, we use basic random vectors representing tree nodes $\vec{n}$. These are generated by independently drawing their elements from a normal distribution N(0,1) with mean 0 and variance 1. The vectors are then normalized so that they have unitary Euclidean length. This generation process guarantees that, for a high enough number of dimensions, the vectors are statistically expected to be nearly orthogonal, i.e. the dot product among pairs of different vectors is expected to be 0.

We can obtain the pure distributed trees (DT) and the distributional distributed trees (DDT) along with their kernel functions, DTK and DDTK, by using different word vectors $\vec{w}$. In the DTs, these vectors are random vectors as the other nodes. In DDTs, these vectors are distributional vectors obtained on a corpus with an LSA reduction (Deerwester et al., 1990).

3.2.1 Entailment-specific Kernels

Recognizing textual entailment (RTE) is a complex semantic task often interpreted as a classification task. Given the text T and the hypothesis H determine whether or not T entails H. For applying the previous kernels to this classification task, we need to define a specific class of kernels. As in (Zanzotto and Moschitti, 2006; Wang and Neumann, 2007; Zanzotto et al., 2009), we encode the text T and the hypothesis H in two separate syntactic feature spaces. Then, given two pairs of text-hypothesis $P_1 = (T_1, H_1)$ and $P_2 = (T_2, H_2)$, the prototypical kernel PK is written as follows:

$$PK(P_1, P_2) = K(T_1, T_2) + K(H_1, H_2) \quad (5)$$

where $K(\cdot, \cdot)$ is a generic kernel. We will then experiment with different PK kernels obtained using: the original tree kernel function (TK) (Collins and Duffy, 2002), DTK, and DDTK.

Along with the previous task specific kernels, we use a simpler feature (Lex) that is extremely effective in determining the entailment between T and H. This simple feature is the lexical similarity between T and H computed using WordNet-based metrics as in (Corley and Mihalcea, 2005). This feature, hereafter called *Lex*, encodes the similarity between T and H, i.e., $sim(T, H)$. This feature is used alone or in combination with the previous kernels and it gives an important boost to their performances. In the task experiment, we will then also have: Lex+TK, Lex+DTK, and Lex+DDTK.

4 Experimental Evaluation

In this section, we experiment with the distributed tree kernels (DTK) and the distributional distributed tree kernels (DDTK) in order to understand whether or not the syntactic structure and the distributional meaning can be easily encoded in the distributed trees. We will experiment in two ways: (1) direct comparison of the distances produced by the original tree kernel (TK) (Collins and Duffy, 2002) and the novel kernels DTK and DDTK; (2) task driven evaluation of DTK and DDTK using the RTE task.

The rest of the section is organized as follows. We firstly introduce the experiment set up that is used for the two settings (Sec. 4.1). Secondly, we report on the experimental results (Sec. 4.2).

4.1 Experimental Set-up

We have the double aim of producing a direct comparison of how the distributed tree kernel (DTK) is approximating the original tree kernel (TK) and a task based comparison for assessing if the approximation is enough effective to similarly solve the task that is textual entailment recognition. For both experimental settings, we take the recognizing textual entailment sets ranging from the first challenge (RTE-1) to the fifth (RTE-5) (Dagan et al., 2006; Bar-Haim et al., 2006; Giampiccolo et al., 2007; Bentivogli et al., 2009).

The distributional vectors used for DDTK have been obtained by an LSA reduction of the word-by-word cooccurrence matrix generated on the UKWaC corpus (Ferraresi et al., 2008), using a context window of size 3. An appropriate size for the LSA reduction was deemed to be 250. Thus, in the experiments we used 250 dimensions both for distributional and random vectors, to allow a correct comparison between DTK and DDTK models.

For the direct comparison, we used tree pairs derived from the RTE sets. Each pair is derived from a T-H pair where T and H are syntactically analyzed and each RTE set produces the corresponding set of tree pairs, e.g., the development set of RTE1 produces a set of 567 tree pairs. To determine whether or not a distributed kernel, DTK or DDTK, is behaving similarly to the original TK kernel, given a set of tree pairs, we produce two ranked lists of tree pairs: the first is ranked according to the original TK applied to the tree pairs and the second according to the target distributed kernel. We evaluate the correlation of the two ranked lists according to the spearman's correlation. Higher correlation corresponds to a better approximation of TK.

For the task driven comparison, we experimented with the datasets in the classical learning setting: the development set is used as training set and the final classifier is tested on the testing set. We used a support vector machine (Joachims, 1999) with an implementation of the original tree kernel (Moschitti, 2006). The classifiers are evaluated according to the accuracy of the classification decision on the testing set, i.e., the ratio of the correct decisions over all the decisions to take.

	Average Spearman's Correlation
DTK	0.8335
$DDTK$	0.7641

Table 1: Average Spearman's correlations of the tree kernel (TK) with the distributed tree kernel (DTK) and the distributed distributional tree kernel (DDTK) in a vector space with 250 dimensions

	avg	RTE1	RTE2	RTE3	RTE5
TK	55.02%	55.50%	53.38%	55.88%	55.33%
DTK	55.63%	57.25%	54.88%	54.38%	56.00%
DDTK	55.11%	54.00%	53.88%	55.38%	57.17%
Lex+TK	62.11%	59.75%	61.25%	66.62%	60.83%
Lex+DTK	63.25%	61.12%	62.12%	66.25%	63.50%
Lex+DDTK	62.90%	60.62%	61.25%	66.38%	63.33%

Table 2: Accuracies of the different methods on the textual entailment recognition task

4.2 Experimental results

In the first experiment of this set, we want to investigate which one between DTK and DDTK correlates better with original TK. Table 1 reports the spearman's correlations of tree kernels with DTK and DDTK in a vector space with 250 dimensions. These correlations are obtained averaging the correlations over the 9 RTE sets. According to these results, DTK better correlates with TK with respect to DDTK. Distributional vectors used for words are not orthogonal as these are used to induce the similarity between words. Yet, this important feature of these vectors determines a worse encoding of the syntactic structure.

In the task driven experiment, we wanted to investigate whether the difference in correlation has some effect on the performance of the different systems. Accuracy results on the RTE task are reported in Table 2. The columns RTE1, RTE2, RTE3, and RTE5 represent the accuracies of the different kernels using the traditional split of training and testing. The column avg reports the average accuracy of the different methods in the 4 sets. Rows represent the different kernels used in this comparative experiment. These kernels are used with the task specific kernel PK by changing the generic kernel K. The first 3 rows represent the *pure* kernels while the last 3 rows represent the kernels boosted with the lexical similarity (Lex), a simple feature computed using WordNet-based metrics, as in (Corley and Mihalcea, 2005). Looking at the first 3 rows, we derive that there is not a significant difference between TK, DTK, and DDTK. DTK and DDTK can then be used instead of the TK. This is an important result, since the computation of DTK (or DDTK) is much faster than that of TK, due to TK's complexity being quadratic with respect to the size of the trees, and DTK requiring a simple dot product over vectors that can be obtained with linear complexity with respect to the tree size. The second fact is that there is no difference between DTK and DDTK: more semantically informed word vectors have the same performance of random vectors.

5 Conclusions

Distributed structures and distributional meaning are largely correlated. In this paper, we analyzed this correlation with respect to the research challenge of producing compositional models for distributional semantics. In the studies of distributed representation, compositionality is a big issue that has produced many models and approaches. Compositional distributional semantics poses the same issue. We empirically showed that a methodology for including distributional meaning in distributed representation is possible, but it must be furtherly developed to be an added value. Distributional semantics has been positively added in traditional tree kernels (Mehdad et al., 2010). Yet, the specific requirement of distributed tree kernels (i.e., the orthogonality of the vectors) reduces this positive effect.

References

James A. Anderson. 1973. A theory for the recognition of items from short memorized lists. *Psychological Review*, 80(6):417 – 438.

Mark Andrews, Gabriella Vigliocco, and David Vinson. 2009. Integrating experiential and distributional data to learn semantic representations. *Psychological Review*, 116(3):463 – 498.

Roy Bar-Haim, Ido Dagan, Bill Dolan, Lisa Ferro, Danilo Giampiccolo, Bernardo Magnini, and Idan Szpektor. 2006. The second pascal recognising textual entailment challenge. In *Proceedings of the Second PASCAL Challenges Workshop on Recognising Textual Entailment*. Venice, Italy.

Marco Baroni and Roberto Zamparelli. 2010. Nouns are vectors, adjectives are matrices: Representing adjective-noun constructions in semantic space. In *Proceedings of the 2010 Conference on Empirical Methods in Natural Language Processing*, pages 1183–1193, Cambridge, MA, October. Association for Computational Linguistics.

Luisa Bentivogli, Ido Dagan, Hoa T. Dang, Danilo Giampiccolo, and Bernardo Magnini. 2009. The Fifth PASCAL Recognizing Textual Entailment Challenge. In *Proceedings of TAC'2009*.

Michael Collins and Nigel Duffy. 2002. New ranking algorithms for parsing and tagging: Kernels over discrete structures, and the voted perceptron. In *Proceedings of ACL02*.

Courtney Corley and Rada Mihalcea. 2005. Measuring the semantic similarity of texts. In *Proc. of the ACL Workshop on Empirical Modeling of Semantic Equivalence and Entailment*, pages 13–18. Association for Computational Linguistics, Ann Arbor, Michigan, June.

Ido Dagan, Oren Glickman, and Bernardo Magnini. 2006. The pascal recognising textual entailment challenge. In Quionero-Candela et al., editor, *LNAI 3944: MLCW 2005*, pages 177–190. Springer-Verlag, Milan, Italy.

Scott C. Deerwester, Susan T. Dumais, Thomas K. Landauer, George W. Furnas, and Richard A. Harshman. 1990. Indexing by latent semantic analysis. *Journal of the American Society of Information Science*, 41(6):391–407.

Adriano Ferraresi, Eros Zanchetta, Marco Baroni, and Silvia Bernardini. 2008. Introducing and evaluating ukwac, a very large web-derived corpus of english. In *In Proceed-ings of the WAC4 Workshop at LREC 2008*, Marrakesh, Morocco.

P. Foltz, W. Kintsch, and T. Landauer. 1998. The measurement of textual coherence with latent semantic analysis. *Discourse Processes*, 25(2&3):285–307.

Gottlob Frege. 1884. *Die Grundlagen der Arithmetik (The Foundations of Arithmetic): eine logisch-mathematische Untersuchung ber den Begriff der Zahl*. Breslau.

Danilo Giampiccolo, Bernardo Magnini, Ido Dagan, and Bill Dolan. 2007. The third pascal recognizing textual entailment challenge. In *Proceedings of the ACL-PASCAL Workshop on Textual Entailment and Paraphrasing*, pages 1–9. Association for Computational Linguistics, Prague, June.

Emiliano Guevara. 2010. A regression model of adjective-noun compositionality in distributional semantics. In *Proceedings of the 2010 Workshop on GEometrical Models of Natural Language Semantics*, pages 33–37, Uppsala, Sweden, July. Association for Computational Linguistics.

G. E. Hinton, J. L. McClelland, and D. E. Rumelhart. 1986. Distributed representations. In D. E. Rumelhart and J. L. McClelland, editors, *Parallel Distributed Processing: Explorations in the Microstructure of Cognition. Volume 1: Foundations*. MIT Press, Cambridge, MA.

Thorsten Joachims. 1999. Making large-scale svm learning practical. In B. Schlkopf, C. Burges, and A. Smola, editors, *Advances in Kernel Methods-Support Vector Learning*. MIT Press.

Thomas K. Landauer and Susan T. Dumais. 1997. A solution to plato's problem: The latent semantic analysis theory of acquisition, induction, and representation of knowledge. *Psychological Review*, 104(2):211–240, April.

K. McRae, V. R. de Sa, and M. S. Seidenberg. 1997. On the nature and scope of featural representations of word meaning. *J Exp Psychol Gen*, 126(2):99–130, June.

Yashar Mehdad, Alessandro Moschitti, and Fabio Massimo Zanzotto. 2010. Syntactic/semantic structures for textual entailment recognition. In *Human Language Technologies: The 2010 Annual Conference of the North American Chapter of the Association for Computational Linguistics*, HLT '10, pages 1020–1028, Stroudsburg, PA, USA. Association for Computational Linguistics.

Jeff Mitchell and Mirella Lapata. 2010. Composition in distributional models of semantics. *Cognitive Science*.

Richard Montague. 1974. English as a formal language. In Richmond Thomason, editor, *Formal Philosophy: Selected Papers of Richard Montague*, pages 188–221. Yale University Press, New Haven.

Alessandro Moschitti. 2006. Making tree kernels practical for natural language learning. In *Proceedings of EACL'06*, Trento, Italy.

Bennet B. Murdock. 1983. A distributed memory model for serial-order information. *Psychological Review*, 90(4):316 – 338.

T. A. Plate. 1994. *Distributed Representations and Nested Compositional Structure*. Ph.D. thesis.

David E. Rumelhart and James L. Mcclelland. 1986. *Parallel Distributed Processing: Explorations in the Microstructure of Cognition : Foundations (Parallel Distributed Processing)*. MIT Press, August.

Vladimir Vapnik. 1995. *The Nature of Statistical Learning Theory*. Springer.

Rui Wang and Günter Neumann. 2007. Recognizing textual entailment using sentence similarity based on dependency tree skeletons. In *Proceedings of the ACL-PASCAL Workshop on Textual Entailment and Paraphrasing*, pages 36–41, Prague, June. Association for Computational Linguistics.

Fabio Massimo Zanzotto and Alessandro Moschitti. 2006. Automatic learning of textual entailments with cross-pair similarities. In *Proceedings of the 21st Coling and 44th ACL*, pages 401–408, Sydney, Australia, July.

Fabio Massimo Zanzotto, Marco Pennacchiotti, and Alessandro Moschitti. 2009. A machine learning approach to textual entailment recognition. *NATURAL LANGUAGE ENGINEERING*, 15-04:551–582.

Fabio Massimo Zanzotto, Ioannis Korkontzelos, Francesca Fallucchi, and Suresh Manandhar. 2010. Estimating linear models for compositional distributional semantics. In *Proceedings of the 23rd International Conference on Computational Linguistics (COLING)*, August,.

Two Multivariate Generalizations of Pointwise Mutual Information

Tim Van de Cruys
RCEAL
University of Cambridge
United Kingdom
tv234@cam.ac.uk

Abstract

Since its introduction into the NLP community, pointwise mutual information has proven to be a useful association measure in numerous natural language processing applications such as collocation extraction and word space models. In its original form, it is restricted to the analysis of two-way co-occurrences. NLP problems, however, need not be restricted to two-way co-occurrences; often, a particular problem can be more naturally tackled when formulated as a multi-way problem. In this paper, we explore two multivariate generalizations of pointwise mutual information, and explore their usefulness and nature in the extraction of *subject verb object* triples.

1 Introduction

Mutual information (Shannon and Weaver, 1949) is a measure of mutual dependence between two random variables. The measure – and more specifically its instantiation for specific outcomes called pointwise mutual information (PMI) – has proven to be a useful association measure in numerous natural language processing applications. Since its introduction into the NLP community (Church and Hanks, 1990), it has been used in order to tackle or improve upon several NLP problems, including collocation extraction (ibid.) and word space models (Pantel and Lin, 2002). In its original form, it is restricted to the analysis of two-way co-occurrences. NLP problems, however, need not be restricted to two-way co-occurrences; often, a particular problem can be more naturally tackled when formulated as a multi-way problem. Notably, the framework of tensor decomposition, that has recently permeated into the NLP community (Turney, 2007; Baroni and Lenci, 2010; Giesbrecht, 2010; Van de Cruys, 2010), analyzes language issues as multi-way co-occurrences. Up till now, little attention has been devoted to the weighting of such multi-way co-occurrences (which, for the research cited above, results either in using no weighting at all, or in applying an ad-hoc weighting solution without any theoretical underpinnings).

In this paper, we explore two possible generalizations of pointwise mutual information for multi-way co-occurrences from a theoretical point of view. In section 2, we discuss some relevant related work, mainly in the field of information theory. In section 3 the two generalizations of PMI are laid out in more detail, based on their global multivariate counterparts. Section 4 then discusses some applications in the light of NLP, while section 5 concludes and hints at some directions for future research.

2 Previous work

Research into the generalization of mutual information was pioneered in two seminal papers. The first one to explore the interaction of multiple random variables in the scope of information theory was McGill (1954). McGill described a first generalization of mutual information based on the notion of conditional entropy. This first generalization, called *interaction information*, is described in section 3.2.1 below. A second generalization, solely based on the commonalities of the random variables, was described by Watanabe (1960). This generalization,

Proceedings of the Workshop on Distributional Semantics and Compositionality (DiSCo'2011), pages 16–20,

called *total correlation* is presented in section 3.2.2.

3 Theory

3.1 Mutual information

Mutual information is a measure of the amount of information that one random variable contains about another random variable. It is the reduction in the uncertainty of one random variable due to the knowledge of the other.

$$I(X;Y) = \sum_{x \in X} \sum_{y \in Y} p(x,y) \log \frac{p(x,y)}{p(x)p(y)} \quad (1)$$

Pointwise mutual information is a measure of association that looks at particular instances of the two random variables X and Y. More specifically, pointwise mutual information measures the difference between the probability of their co-occurrence given their joint distribution and the probability of their co-occurrence given the marginal distributions of X and Y (thus assuming the two random variables are independent).

$$pmi(x,y) = \log \frac{p(x,y)}{p(x)p(y)} \quad (2)$$

Note that mutual information (equation 1) yields the expected PMI value over all possible instances of random variables X and Y.

$$\mathbb{E}_{p(X,Y)}[pmi(X,Y)] \quad (3)$$

Furthermore, note that PMI may be positive or negative, but its expected outcome over all events (i.e. the global mutual information) is always non-negative.

3.2 Multivariate mutual information

In this section, the two generalizations for multivariate distributions are presented. For both generalizations, we examine their standard form (which looks at the interaction between the random variables as a whole) and their specific instantiation (that looks at particular outcomes of the random variables). Analogously to PMI, it is these specific instantiations of the measures that are able to weigh specific co-occurrences according to their importance in the corpus. As with PMI, the value for the global case ought to be the expected value for all the instantiations of the specific measure.

3.2.1 Interaction information

Interaction information (McGill, 1954) – also called co-information (Bell, 2003) – is based on the notion of conditional mutual information. Conditional mutual information is the mutual information of two random variables conditioned on a third one.

$$\begin{aligned} &I(X;Y|Z) \\ &= \sum_{x \in X} \sum_{y \in Y} \sum_{z \in Z} p(x,y,z) \log \frac{p(x,y|z)}{p(x|z)p(y|z)} \end{aligned} \quad (4)$$

which can be rewritten as

$$\sum_{x \in X} \sum_{y \in Y} \sum_{z \in Z} p(x,y,z) \log \frac{p(z)p(x,y,z)}{p(x,z)p(y,z)} \quad (5)$$

For the case of three variables, the interaction information is then defined as the conditional mutual information subtracted by the standard mutual information.

$$\begin{aligned} I_1(X;Y;Z) &= I(X;Y|Z) - I(X;Y) \\ &= I(X;Z|Y) - I(X;Z) \\ &= I(Y;Z|X) - I(Y;Z) \end{aligned} \quad (6)$$

Expanded, this gives the following equation:

$$\begin{aligned} &I_1(X;Y;Z) \\ &= \sum_{x \in X} \sum_{y \in Y} \sum_{z \in Z} p(x,y,z) \log \frac{p(z)p(x,y,z)}{p(x,z)p(y,z)} \\ &\quad - \sum_{x \in X} \sum_{y \in Y} p(x,y) \log \frac{p(x,y)}{p(x)p(y)} \end{aligned} \quad (7)$$

We can now define *specific interaction information* as follows[1]:

[1]Note that – compared to equation 7 – the two subparts in the right-hand side of the equation have been swapped. For the three-variable case, this gives exactly the same outcome except for a change in sign. The swap is necessary in order to ensure a proper set-theoretic measure (Fano, 1961; Reza, 1994).

$$SI_1(x,y,z) = \log \frac{p(x,y)}{p(x)p(y)} - \log \frac{p(z)p(x,y,z)}{p(x,z)p(y,z)} = \log \frac{p(x,y)p(y,z)p(x,z)}{p(x)p(y)p(z)p(x,y,z)} \quad (8)$$

Interaction information – as well as specific interaction information – can equally be defined for $n > 3$ variables.

3.2.2 Total correlation

Total correlation (Watanabe, 1960) – also called multi-information (Studený and Vejnarová, 1998) quantifies the amount of information that is shared among the different random variables, and thus expresses how related a particular group of random variables are.

$$I_2(X_1, X_2, \ldots, X_n) = \sum_{\substack{x_1 \in X_1, \\ x_2 \in X_2, \\ \ldots \\ x_n \in X_n}} p(x_1, x_2, \ldots, x_n) \log \frac{p(x_1, x_2, \ldots, x_n)}{\Pi_{i=1}^n p(x_i)} \quad (9)$$

Analogously to the definition of pointwise mutual information, we can straightforwardly define the correlation for specific instances of the random variables, which we coin *specific correlation*.

$$SI_2(x_1, x_2, \ldots, x_n) = \log \frac{p(x_1, x_2, \ldots, x_n)}{\Pi_{i=1}^n p(x_i)} \quad (10)$$

For the case of three variables, this gives the following equation:

$$SI_2(x,y,z) = \log \frac{p(x,y,z)}{p(x)p(y)p(z)} \quad (11)$$

Note that this measure has been used in NLP tasks before, notably for collocation extraction (Villada Moirón, 2005).

4 Application

In this section, we explore the performance of the measures defined above in an NLP context, viz. the extraction of salient *subject verb object* triples. This research has been carried out for Dutch. The Twente Nieuws Corpus (Ordelman, 2002), a 500M Dutch word corpus, has been automatically parsed with the Dutch dependency parser ALPINO (van Noord, 2006), and all *subject verb object* triples with frequency $f \geq 3$ have been extracted. Next, a tensor $\mathcal{T}$ of size $I \times J \times K$ has been constructed, containing the three-way co-occurrence frequencies of the I most frequent subjects by the J most frequent verbs by the K most frequent objects, with $I = 10000, J = 1000, K = 10000$. Finally, two new tensors $\mathcal{U}$ and $\mathcal{V}$ have been constructed, such that $\mathcal{U}_{ijk} = SI_1(\mathcal{T}_{ijk})$ and $\mathcal{V}_{ijk} = SI_2(\mathcal{T}_{ijk})$, i.e. tensor $\mathcal{U}$ has been weighted using specific interaction information (equation 8) and tensor $\mathcal{V}$ has been weighted using specific correlation (equation 11).

Table 1 shows the top five *subject verb object* triples that received the highest specific interaction information score, while table 2 gives the top five *subject verb object* triples that gained the highest specific correlation score (both with $f > 30$).

Note that both methods are able to extract salient *subject verb object* triples, such as prototypical *svo* combinations (*peiling geeft opinie weer* 'poll represents opinion', *helikopter vuurt raket af* 'helicopter fires rocket') and fixed expressions (Dutch proverbs such as *de wal keert het schip* 'the circumstances change the course' and *de vlag dekt de lading* 'the content corresponds to the title').

subject	verb	object	SI_1
peiling	*geef weer*	*opinie*	18.20
'poll'	'represent'	'opinion'	
helikopter	*vuur af*	*raket*	17.57
'helicopter'	'fire'	'rocket'	
Man	*bijt*	*hond*	17.15
'man'	'bite'	'dog'	
verwijt	*snijd*	*hout*	17.10
'reproach'	'cut'	'wood'	
wal	*keer*	*schip*	17.01
'quay'	'turn'	'ship'	

Table 1: Top five *subject verb object* triples with highest *specific interaction information* score

Comparing both methods, the results seem to indicate that the extracted triples are similar for both weightings. This, however, is not consistently the case: the results can differ significantly for partic-

subject	verb	object	SI_2
verwijt	*snijd*	*hout*	8.05
'reproach'	'cut'	'wood'	
helikopter	*vuur af*	*raket*	7.75
'helicopter'	'fire'	'rocket'	
peiling	*geef weer*	*opinie*	7.64
'poll'	'represent'	'opinion'	
vlag	*dek*	*lading*	7.21
'flag'	'cover'	'load'	
argument	*snijd*	*hout*	7.17
'argument'	'cut'	'wood'	

Table 2: Top five *subject verb object* triples with highest *specific correlation* score

ular instances. This becomes apparent when comparing table 3 and table 4, which for each method contain the top five combinations for the Dutch verb *speel* 'play'.

Table 3 indicates that specific interaction information picks up on prototypical *svo* combinations (*orkest speelt symfonie* 'orchestra plays symphony'; also note the 4 other triples that come from bridge game descriptions). Specific correlation (table 4), on the other hand, picks up on the expression *een rol spelen* 'play a role', and extracts salient subjects that go with the expression.

subject	verb	object	SI_1
orkest	*speel*	*symfonie*	11.65
'orchestra'	'play'	'symphony'	
leider	*speel*	*ruiten*	10.29
'leader'	'play'	'diamonds'	
leider	*speel*	*harten*	10.20
'leader'	'play'	'hearts'	
leider	*speel*	*schoppen*	10.01
'leader'	'play'	'spades'	
leider	*speel*	*klaveren*	9.89
'leader'	'play'	'clubs'	

Table 3: Top five combinations with highest *specific interaction information* scores for verb *speel*

In order to quantitatively assess the aptness of the two methods for the extraction of salient *svo* triples, we performed a small-scale manual evaluation of the 100 triples that scored the highest for each measure.

subject	verb	object	SI_2
nationaliteit	*speel*	*rol*	4.12
'nationality'	'play'	'role'	
afkomst	*speel*	*rol*	4.06
'descent'	'play'	'role'	
toeval	*speel*	*rol*	4.04
'coincidence'	'play'	'role'	
motief	*speel*	*rol*	4.04
'motive'	'play'	'role'	
afstand	*speel*	*rol*	4.02
'distance'	'play'	'role'	

Table 4: Top five combinations with highest *specific correlation* scores for verb *speel*

A triple is considered salient when it is made up of a fixed (multi-word) expression, or when it consists of a fixed expression combined with a salient subject or object (e.g. *argument snijd hout* 'argument cut wood'). The bare frequency tensor (without any weighting) was used as a baseline. The results are presented in table 5.

measure	precision
baseline	.00
SI_1	.24
SI_2	.31

Table 5: Manual evaluation results for the extraction of salient *svo* triples

The results indicate that both measures are able to extract a significant number of salient triples compared to the frequency baseline, which is not able to extract any salient triples at all. Comparing both measures, *specific correlation* clearly performs best (.31 versus .24 for *specific interaction information*).

Additionally, we computed Kendall's τ_b to compare the rankings yielded by the two different methods (over all triples). The correlation between both rankings is $\tau_b = 0.21$, indicating that the results yielded by both methods – though correlated – differ to a significant extent.

These are, of course, preliminary results, and a more thorough evaluation is necessary to confirm the tendencies that emerge.

5 Conclusion

In this paper, we presented two multivariate generalizations of mutual information, as well as their instantiated counterparts *specific interaction information* and *specific correlation*, that are useful for weighting multi-way co-occurrences in NLP tasks. The main goal of this paper is to show that there is not just one straightforward generalization of pointwise mutual information for the multivariate case, and NLP researchers that want to exploit multi-way co-occurrences in an information-theoretic framework should take this fact into account.

Moreover, we have applied the two different measures to the extraction of *subject verb object* triples, and demonstrated that the results may differ significantly. It goes without saying that these are just exploratory and rudimentary observations; more research into the exact nature of both generalizations and their repercussions for NLP – as well as a proper quantitative evaluation – are imperative.

This brings us to some avenues for future work. More research needs to be carried with regard to the exact nature of the dependencies that both measures capture. Preliminary results show that they extract different information, but it is not clear what the exact nature of that information is. Secondly, we want to carry out a proper quantitative evaluation on different multi-way co-occurrence (factorization) tasks, in order to indicate which measure works best, and which measure might be more suitable for a particular task.

Acknowledgements

A number of anonymous reviewers provided fruitful remarks and comments on an earlier draft of this paper, from which the current version has significantly benefited.

References

Marco Baroni and Alessandro Lenci. 2010. Distributional memory: A general framework for corpus-based semantics. *Computational Linguistics*, 36(4):1–48.

Anthony J. Bell. 2003. The co-information lattice. In *Proceedings of the Fifth International Workshop on Independent Component Analysis and Blind Signal Separation: ICA 2003*.

Kenneth W. Church and Patrick Hanks. 1990. Word association norms, mutual information & lexicography. *Computational Linguistics*, 16(1):22–29.

Robert Fano. 1961. *Transmission of information*. MIT Press, Cambridge, MA.

Eugenie Giesbrecht. 2010. Towards a matrix-based distributional model of meaning. In *Proceedings of the NAACL HLT 2010 Student Research Workshop*, pages 23–28. Association for Computational Linguistics.

William J. McGill. 1954. Multivariate information transmission. *Psychometrika*, 19(2):97–116.

R.J.F. Ordelman. 2002. Twente Nieuws Corpus (TwNC), August. Parlevink Language Techonology Group. University of Twente.

Patrick Pantel and Dekang Lin. 2002. Discovering word senses from text. In *Proceedings of ACM Conference on Knowledge Discovery and Data Mining*, pages 613–619, Edmonton, Canada.

Fazlollah M. Reza. 1994. *An introduction to information theory*. Dover Publications.

Claude Shannon and Warren Weaver. 1949. *The mathematical theory of communication*. University of Illinois Press, Urbana, Illinois.

M. Studený and J. Vejnarová. 1998. The multiinformation function as a tool for measuring stochastic dependence. In *Proceedings of the NATO Advanced Study Institute on Learning in graphical models*, pages 261–297, Norwell, MA, USA. Kluwer Academic Publishers.

Peter D. Turney. 2007. Empirical evaluation of four tensor decomposition algorithms. Technical Report ERB-1152, National Research Council, Institute for Information Technology.

Tim Van de Cruys. 2010. A non-negative tensor factorization model for selectional preference induction. *Natural Language Engineering*, 16(4):417–437.

Gertjan van Noord. 2006. At Last Parsing Is Now Operational. In Piet Mertens, Cedrick Fairon, Anne Dister, and Patrick Watrin, editors, *TALN06. Verbum Ex Machina. Actes de la 13e conference sur le traitement automatique des langues naturelles*, pages 20–42, Leuven.

Begoña Villada Moirón. 2005. *Data-driven identification of fixed expressions and their modifiability*. Ph.D. thesis, University of Groningen, The Netherlands.

Satosi Watanabe. 1960. Information theoretical analysis of multivariate correlation. *IBM Journal of Research and Development*, 4:66–82.

Distributional Semantics and Compositionality 2011: Shared Task Description and Results

Chris Biemann
UKP lab, Technical University of Darmstadt
Hochschulstr. 10
64289 Darmstadt, Germany
biemann@tk.informatik.tu-darmstadt.de

Eugenie Giesbrecht
FZI Forschungszentrum Informatik
Haid-und-Neu-Str. 10-14
76131 Karlsruhe, Germany
giesbrecht@fzi.de

Abstract

This paper gives an overview of the shared task at the ACL-HLT 2011 DiSCo (Distributional Semantics and Compositionality) workshop. We describe in detail the motivation for the shared task, the acquisition of datasets, the evaluation methodology and the results of participating systems. The task of assigning a numerical score for a phrase according to its compositionality showed to be hard. Many groups reported features that intuitively should work, yet showed no correlation with the training data. The evaluation reveals that most systems outperform simple baselines, yet have difficulties in reliably assigning a compositionality score that closely matches the gold standard. Overall, approaches based on word space models performed slightly better than methods relying solely on statistical association measures.

1 Introduction

Any NLP system that does semantic processing relies on the assumption of semantic compositionality: the meaning of a phrase is determined by the meanings of its parts and their combination. However, this assumption does not hold for lexicalized phrases such as idiomatic expressions, which causes troubles not only for semantic, but also for syntactic processing (Sag et al., 2002). In particular, while distributional methods in semantics have proved to be very efficient in tackling a wide range of tasks in natural language processing, e.g., document retrieval, clustering and classification, question answering, query expansion, word similarity, synonym extraction, relation extraction, textual advertisement matching in search engines, etc. (see Turney and Pantel (2010) for a detailed overview), they are still strongly limited by being inherently word-based. While dictionaries and other lexical resources contain multiword entries, these are expensive to obtain and not available for all languages to a sufficient extent. Furthermore, the definition of a multiword varies across resources, and non-compositional phrases are often merely a subclass of multiword units.

This shared task addressed researchers that are interested in extracting non-compositional phrases from large corpora by applying distributional models that assign a graded compositionality score to a phrase, as well as researchers interested in expressing compositional meaning with such models. The score denotes the extent to which the compositionality assumption holds for a given expression. The latter can be used, for example, to decide whether the phrase should be treated as a single unit in applications. We emphasized that the focus is on automatically acquiring semantic compositionality and explicitly did not invite approaches that employ prefabricated lists of non-compositional phrases.

It is often the case that compositionality of a phrase depends on the context. Though we have used a sentence context in the process of constructing the gold standard, we have decided not to provide it with the dataset: we have asked for a single compositionality score per phrase. In an application, this could play the role of a compositionality prior that could, e.g., be stored in a dictionary. There is a long-living tradition within the research

Proceedings of the Workshop on Distributional Semantics and Compositionality (DiSCo'2011), pages 21–28,
Portland, Oregon, 24 June 2011.

community working on multiword units (MWUs) to automatically classify MWUs into either compositional or non-compositional ones. However, it has been often noted that compositionality comes in degrees, and a binary classification is not valid enough in many cases (Bannard et al., 2003; Katz and Giesbrecht, 2006). To the best of our knowledge, this has been the first attempt to offer a dataset and a shared task that allows to explicitly evaluate the models of graded compositionality.

2 Shared Task Description

For the shared task, we aimed to get compositionality scores for phrases frequently occurring in corpora. Since distributional models need large corpora to perform reliable statistics, and these statistics are more reliable for frequent items, we chose to restrict the candidate set to the most frequent phrases from the freely available WaCky[1] web corpora (Baroni et al., 2009). Those are currently downloadable for English, French, German and Italian. They have already been automatically sentence-split, tokenized, part-of-speech (POS) tagged and lemmatized, which reduces the load on both organizers and participants that decide to make use of these corpora. Further, WaCky corpora provide a good starting point for experimenting with distributional models due to their size, ranging between 1-2 billion tokens, and extensive efforts to make these corpora as clean as possible.

2.1 Candidate Selection

There is a wide range of subsentential units that can function as a non-compositional construction. These units do not have to be realized continuously in the surface realization and can consist of an arbitrary number of lexical items. While it would be interesting to examine unrestricted forms of multiwords and compositional phrases, we decided to restrict candidate selection to certain grammatical constructions to make the task more tangible. Specifically, we use word pairs in the following relations:

- ADJ_NN: Adjective modifying a noun, e.g. "red herring" or "blue skies"
- V_SUBJ: Noun in subject position and verb, e..g. "flies fly" or "people transfer (sth.)"
- V_OBJ: Noun in object position and verb, e.g. "lose keys", "play song"

While it is possible to extract the relations fairly accurately from parsed English text, there is – to our knowledge – no reliable, freely available method that can tell verb-subjects from verb-objects for German. Thus, we employed a three-step selection procedure for producing a set of candidate phrases per grammatical relation and language that involved heavy manual intervention.

1. Extract candidates using (possibly overgenerating) patterns over part-of-speech sequences and sort by frequency
2. Manually select plausible candidates for the target grammatical relation in order of decreasing frequency
3. Balance the candidate set to select enough non-compositional phrases

For English, we used the following POS patterns: ADJ_NN: "JJ* NN*"; V_SUBJ: "NN* VV*"; V_OBJ: "VV* DT|CD NN*" and "VV* NN*". The star * denotes continuation of tag labels: e.g. VV* matches all tags starting with "VV", such as VV, VVD, VVG, VVN, VVP and VVZ.

For German, we used "ADJ* NN*" for ADJ_NN. For relations involving nouns and verbs, we extracted all noun-verb pairs in a window of 4 tokens and manually filtered by relation on the aggregated frequency list. Frequencies were computed on the lemma forms.

This introduces a bias on the possible constructions that realize the target relations, especially for the verb-noun pairs. Further, the selection procedure is biased by the intuition of the person that performs the selection. We only admitted what we thought were clear-cut cases (only nouns that are typically found in subject respectively object position) to the candidate set at this stage.

Since non-compositional phrases are much less in numbers than compositional phrases, we tried to somewhat balance this in the third step in the selection. If the candidates would have been randomly

[1] http://wacky.sslmit.unibo.it

selected, an overwhelming number of compositional phrases would have rendered the task very hard to evaluate, since a baseline system predicting high compositionality in all cases would have achieved a very high score. We argue that since we are especially interested in non-compositional phrases in this competition, it is valid to bias the dataset in this way.

After we collected a candidate list, we randomly selected seven sentences per candidate from the corpus. Through manual filtering, we checked whether the target word pair was in fact found in the target relation in these sentences. Further we removed incomplete and too long sentences, so that we ended up with five sentences per target phrase. Some candidate phrases that only occurred in very fixed contexts (e.g. disclaimers) or did not have enough well-formed sentences were removed in this step.

Figure 1 shows the sentences for "V_OBJ: buck trend" as an example output of this procedure.

2.2 Annotation

The sample usages of target phrases now had to be annotated for compositionality. We employed the crowdsourcing service Amazon Turk[2] for realizing these annotations. The advantage of crowdsourcing is its scalability through the large numbers of workers that are ready to perform small tasks for pay. The disadvantage is that tasks usually cannot be very complex, since quality issues (scammers) have to be addressed either with test items or redundancy or both – mechanisms that only work for types of tasks where there is clearly a correct answer.

Previous experiences in constructing linguistic annotations with Amazon Turk (Biemann and Nygaard, 2010) made us stick to the following two-step procedure that more or less ensured the quality of annotation by hand-picking workers:

1. *Gather high quality workers*: In an open task for a small data sample with unquestionable decisions, we collected annotations from a large number of workers. Workers were asked to provide reasons for their decisions. Workers that performed well, gave reasons that demonstrated their understanding of the task and completed a significant amount of the examples were invited for a closed task. Net pay was 2 US cents for completing a HIT.

2. *Get annotations for the real task*: In the closed task, only invited workers were admitted and redundancy was reduced to four workers per HIT. Net pay was 3 US cents for completing a HIT.

Figure 2 shows a sample HIT (human intelligence task) for English on Amazon turk, including instructions. Workers were asked to enter a judgment from 0-10 about the literacy of the highlighted target phrase in the respective context. For the German data, we used an equivalent task definition in German.

All five contexts per target phrase were scored by four workers each. A few items were identified as problematic by the workers (e.g. missing highlighting, too little context), and one worker was excluded during the English experiment for starting to deliberately scam. For this worker, all judgments were removed and not repeated. Thus, the standard number of judgments per target phrase was 20, with some targets receiving less judgments because of these problems. The minimum number of judgments per target phrase was 12: four HITs with three judgments each.

From this, we computed a score by averaging over all judgments per phrase and multiplying the overall score by 10 to get scores in the range of 0-100. This score cannot help in discriminating moderately compositional phrases like "V_OBJ: make decision" from phrases that are dependent on the context like "V_OBJ: wait minute" which had two HITs for the idiomatic use of "wait a minute!" and three HITs with literally minutes to spend idling.

As each HIT was annotated by a possibly different set of workers, it is not possible to compute inter-annotator agreement. Eyeballing the scores revealed that some workers generally tend to give higher respectively lower scores than others. Overall, workers agreed more for clearly compositional or clearly non-compositional HITs. We believe that using this comparatively high number of judgments per target, averaged over several contexts, should give us fairly reliable judgments, as worker biases should cancel out each other.

[2]http://www.mturk.com

- I would like to **buck** the **trend** of complaint !
- One company that is **bucking** the **trend** is Flowcrete Group plc located in Sandbach , Cheshire .
- " We are now moving into a new phase where we are hoping to **buck** the **trend** .
- With a claimed 11,000 customers and what look like aggressive growth plans , including recent acquisitions of Infinium Software , Interbiz and earlier also Max international , the firm does seem to be **bucking** the **trend** of difficult times .
- Every time we get a new PocketPC in to Pocket-Lint tower , it seems to offer more features for less money and the HP iPaq 4150 is n't about to **buck** the **trend** .

Figure 1: sentences for V_OBJ: buck trend after manual filtering and selection. The target is **highlighted**.

How literal is this phrase?

Can you infer the meaning of a given phrase by only considering their parts literally, or does the phrase carry a 'special' meaning?
In the context below, how literal is the meaning of the phrase in bold?
Enter a number between 0 and 10.

- 0 means: this phrase is not to be understood literally at all.
- 10 means: this phrase is to be understood very literally.
- Use values in between to grade your decision. Please, however, try to *take a stand as often as possible.*

In case the context is unclear or nonsensical, please enter "66" and use the comment field to explain. However, please try to make sense of it even if the sentences are incomplete.

Example 1 :
There was a red truck parked curbside. It looked like someone was living in it.
YOUR ANSWER: 10
reason: the color of the truck is red, this can be inferred from the parts "red" and "truck" only - without any special knowledge.

? Example 2 :
What a tour! We were on cloud nine when we got back to headquarters but we kept our mouths shut.
YOUR ANSWER: 0
reason: "cloud nine" means to be blissfully happy. It does NOT refer to a cloud with the number nine.

Example 3 :
Yellow fever is found only in parts of South America and Africa.
YOUR ANSWER: 7
reason: "yellow fever" refers to a disease causing high body temperature. However, the fever itself is not yellow. Overall, this phrase is fairly literal, but not totally, hence answering with a value between 5 and 8 is appropriate.

We take rejection seriously and will not reject a HIT unless done carelessly. Entering anything else but numbers between 0 and 10 or 66 in the judgment field will automatically trigger rejection.

YOUR CONTEXT with **big day**
Special Offers : Please call FREEPHONE 0800 0762205 to receive your free copy of ' Groom ' the full colour magazine dedicated to dressing up for the **big day** and details of Moss Bros Hire rates .

How literal is the bolded phrase in the context above between 0 and 10?
[ ]

OPTIONAL: leave a comment, tell us about what is broken, help us to improve this type of HIT:
[ ]

Figure 2: Sample Human Intelligence Task on Amazon Turk with annotation instructions

EN	ADJ_NN	V_SUBJ	V_OBJ	Sum
Train	58 (43)	30 (23)	52 (41)	140 (107)
Vali.	10 (7)	9 (6)	16 (13)	35 (26)
Test	77 (52)	35 (26)	62 (40)	174 (118)
All	145 (102)	74 (55)	130 (94)	349 (251)

Table 1: English dataset: number of target phrases (with coarse scores)

DE	ADJ_NN	V_SUBJ	V_OBJ	Sum
Train	49 (42)	26 (23)	44 (33)	119 (98)
Vali.	11 (8)	9 (8)	9 (7)	29 (23)
Test	63 (48)	29 (28)	57 (44)	149 (120)
All	123 (98)	64 (59)	110 ()	297 (241)

Table 2: German dataset: number of target phrases (with coarse scores)

Additionally to the numerical scores, we've also provided coarse-grained labels. This is motivated by the following: for some applications, it is probably enough to decide whether a phrase is always compositional, somewhat compositional or usually not compositional, without the need of more fine-grained distinctions. For this, we've transformed the numerical scores in the range of 0-25 to coarse label "low", those between 38-62 have been labeled as "medium", and the ones from 75 to 100 have received the value "high". All other phrases have been excluded from the corresponding training and test datasets for "coarse evaluation" (s. Section 2.4.2): 28.1% of English and 18.9% of German phrases.

2.3 Datasets

Now we describe the datasets in detail. Table 1 summarizes the English data, Table 2 describes the German data quantitatively. Per language and relation, the data was randomly split in approximatively 40% training, 10% validation and 50% test.

2.4 Scoring of system responses

We provided evaluation scripts along with the training and validation data. Additionally, we report correlation values (Spearman's rho and Kendall's tau) in Section 4.

2.4.1 Numerical Scoring

For numerical scoring, the evaluation script computes the distance between the system responses $S = \{s_{target1}, s_{target2}, ...s_{targetN}\}$ and the gold standard $G = \{g_{target1}, g_{target2}, ...g_{targetN}\}$ in points, averaged over all items:

$$NUMSCORE(S,G) = \frac{1}{N}\sum_{i=1..N} |g_i - s_i|.$$

Missing values in the system scores are filled with the default value of 50. A perfect score is 0, indicating no difference between the system responses and the gold standard.

2.4.2 Coarse Scoring

We use precision on coarse label predictions for coarse scoring:

$$COARSE(S,G) = \frac{1}{N}\sum_{i=1..N} \begin{cases} s_i == g_i : 1 \\ otherwise : 0 \end{cases}.$$

As with numerical scoring, missing system responses are filled with a default value, in this case 'medium'. A perfect score would be 1.00, connoting complete congruence of gold standard and system response labels.

3 Participants

Seven teams participated in the shared task. Table 3 summarizes the participants and their systems. Four of the teams (Duluth, UoY, JUCSE, SCSS-TCD) submitted three runs for the whole English test set. One team participated with two systems, one of which was for the entire English dataset and another one included entries only for English V_SUBJ and V_OBJ relations. A team from UNED provided scores solely for English ADJ_NN pairs. UCPH was the only team that delivered results for both English and German.

Systems can be split into approaches based on statistical association measures and approaches based on word space models. On top, some systems used a machine-learned classifier to predict numerical scores or coarse labels.

4 Results

The results of the official evaluation for English are shown in Tables 4 and 5.

Table 4 reports the results for numerical scoring. *UCPH-simple.en* performed best with the score of 16.19. The second best system *UoY: Exm-Best* achieved 16.51, and the third was *UoY:Pro-Best* with 16.79. It is worth noting that the top six systems

Systems	Institution	Team	Approach
Duluth-1 Duluth-2 Duluth-3	Dept. of Computer Science, University of Minnesota	Ted Pedersen	statistical association measures: t-score and pmi
JUCSE-1 JUCSE-2 JUCSE-3	Jadavpur University	Tanmoy Chakraborty, Santanu Pal Tapabrata Mondal, Tanik Saikh, Sivaju Bandyopadhyay	mix of statistical association measures
SCSS-TCD:conf1 SCSS-TCD:conf2 SCSS-TCD:conf3	SCSS, Trinity College Dublin	Alfredo Maldonado-Guerra, Martin Emms	unsupervised WSM, cosine similarity
submission-ws submission-pmi	Gavagai	Hillevi Hägglöf, Lisa Tengstrand	random indexing association measures (pmi)
UCPH-simple.en	University of Copenhagen	Anders Johannsen, Hector Martinez, Christian Rishøj, Anders Søgaard	support vector regression with COALS-based endocentricity features
UoY: Exm UoY: Exm-Best UoY: Pro-Best	University of York, UK; Lexical Computing Ltd., UK	Siva Reddy, Diana McCarthy, Suresh Manandhar, Spandana Gella	exemplar-based WSMs prototype-based WSM
UNED-1: NN UNED-2: NN UNED-3: NN	NLP and IR Group at UNED	Guillermo Garrido, Anselmo Peas	syntactic VSM, dependency-parsed UKWaC, SVM classifier

Table 3: Participants of DiSCo'2011 Shared Task

in the numerical evaluation are all based on different variations of word space models.

The outcome of evaluation for coarse scores is displayed in Table 5. Here, *Duluth-1* performs highest with 0.585, followed closely by *UoY:ExmBest with 0.576* and *UoY: ProBest* with 0.567. *Duluth-1* is an approach purely based on association measures.

Both tables also report ZERO-response and RANDOM-response baselines. ZERO-response means that, if no score is reported for a phrase, it gets a default value of 50 (fifty) points in numerical evaluation and 'medium' in coarse evaluation. Random baselines were created by using random labels from a uniform distribution. Most systems beat the RANDOM-response baseline, only about half of the systems are better than ZERO-response.

Apart from the officially announced scoring methods, we provide Spearman's rho and Kendall's tau rank correlations for numerical scoring. Rank correlation scores that are not significant are noted in parentheses. With correlations, the higher the score, the better is the system's ability to order the phrases according to their compositionality scores. Here, systems *UoY: Exm-Best*, *UoY: Pro-Best* / *JUCSE-1* and *JUCSE-2* achieved the first, second and third best results respectively.

Overall, there is no clear winner for the English dataset. However, across different scoring mechanisms, *UoY: Exm-Best* is the most robust of the systems. The *UCPH-simple.en* system has a stellar performance on V_OBJ but apparently uses a suboptimal way of assigning coarse labels. The *Duluth-1* system, on the other hand, is not able to produce a numerical ranking that is significant according to the correlation measures, but excels in the coarse scoring.

When comparing word space models and association measures, it seems that the former do a slightly better job on modeling graded compositionality, which is especially obvious in the numerical evaluation.

Since word space models and statistical association measures are language-independent approaches and most teams have not used syntactic preprocessing other than POS tagging, it is a pity that only one team has tried the German task (see Tables 6 and 7). The comparison to the baselines shows that the *UCPH* system is robust across languages and performs (relatively speaking) equally well in the numerical scoring both for the German and the English tasks.

numerical scores	responses	ρ	τ	EN all	EN_ADJ_NN	EN_V_SUBJ	EN_V_OBJ
number of phrases				174	77	35	62
0-response baseline	0	-	-	23.42	24.67	17.03	25.47
random baseline	174	(0.02)	(0.02)	32.82	34.57	29.83	32.34
UCPH-simple.en	174	0.27	0.18	**16.19**	14.93	21.64	**14.66**
UoY: Exm-Best	169	**0.35**	**0.24**	16.51	15.19	**15.72**	18.6
UoY: Pro-Best	169	0.33	0.23	16.79	**14.62**	18.89	18.31
UoY: Exm	169	0.26	0.18	17.28	15.82	18.18	18.6
SCSS-TCD: conf1	174	0.27	0.19	17.95	18.56	20.8	15.58
SCSS-TCD: conf2	174	0.28	0.19	18.35	19.62	20.2	15.73
Duluth-1	174	(-0.01)	(-0.01)	21.22	19.35	26.71	20.45
JUCSE-1	174	0.33	0.23	22.67	25.32	17.71	22.16
JUCSE-2	174	0.32	0.22	22.94	25.69	17.51	22.6
SCSS-TCD: conf3	174	0.18	0.12	25.59	24.16	32.04	23.73
JUCSE-3	174	(-0.04)	(-0.03)	25.75	30.03	26.91	19.77
Duluth-2	174	(-0.06)	(-0.04)	27.93	37.45	17.74	21.85
Duluth-3	174	(-0.08)	(-0.05)	33.04	44.04	17.6	28.09
submission-ws	173	0.24	0.16	44.27	37.24	50.06	49.72
submission-pmi	96	-	-	-	-	52.13	50.46
UNED-1: NN	77	-	-	-	17.02	-	-
UNED-2: NN	77	-	-	-	17.18	-	-
UNED-3: NN	77	-	-	-	17.29	-	-

Table 4: Numerical evaluation scores for English: average point difference and correlation measures (not significant values in parentheses)

coarse values	responses	EN all	EN_ADJ_NN	EN_V_SUBJ	EN_V_OBJ
number of phrases		118	52	26	40
zero-response baseline	0	0.356	0.288	0.654	0.250
random baseline	118	0.297	0.288	0.308	0.300
Duluth-1	118	**0.585**	0.654	0.385	0.625
UoY: Exm-Best	114	0.576	0.692	0.500	0.475
UoY: Pro-Best	114	0.567	**0.731**	0.346	0.500
UoY: Exm	114	0.542	0.692	0.346	0.475
SCSS-TCD: conf2	118	0.542	0.635	0.192	**0.650**
SCSS-TCD: conf1	118	0.534	0.64	0.192	0.625
JUCSE-3	118	0.475	0.442	0.346	0.600
JUCSE-2	118	0.458	0.481	0.462	0.425
SCSS-TCD: conf3	118	0.449	0.404	0.423	0.525
JUCSE-1	118	0.441	0.442	0.462	0.425
submission-ws	117	0.373	0.346	0.269	0.475
UCPH-simple.en	118	0.356	0.346	0.500	0.275
Duluth-2	118	0.322	0.173	0.346	0.500
Duluth-3	118	0.322	0.135	**0.577**	0.400
submission-pmi	-	-	-	0.346	0.550
UNED-1-NN	52	-	0.289	-	-
UNED-2-NN	52	-	0.404	-	-
UNED-3-NN	52	-	0.327	-	-

Table 5: Coarse evaluation scores for English

numerical scores	responses	ρ	τ	DE all	DE_ADJ_NN	DE_V_SUBJ	DE_V_OBJ
number of phrases				149	63	29	57
0-response baseline	0	-	-	32.51	32.21	38.00	30.05
random baseline	149	(0.005)	(0.004)	37.79	36.27	47.45	34.54
UCPH-simple.de	148	0.171	0.116	24.03	27.09	15.55	24.06

Table 6: Numerical evaluation scores for German

heightcoarse values	responses	DE all	DE_ADJ_NN	DE_V_SUBJ	DE_V_OBJ
number of phrases		120	48	28	44
0-response baseline	0	0.158	0.208	0.071	0.159
random baseline	120	0.283	0.313	0.214	0.295
UCPH-simple.de	119	0.283	0.375	0.286	0.182

Table 7: Coarse evaluation scores for German

For more details on the systems as well as fine-grained analysis of the results, please consult the corresponding system description papers.

5 Conclusion

DiSCo Shared Task attracted seven groups that submitted results for 19 systems. We consider this a success, taking into consideration that the task is new and difficult. The opportunity to evaluate language-independent models for languages other than English was unfortunately not taken up by most participants.

The teams applied a variety of approaches that can be classified into lexical association measures and word space models of various flavors. From the evaluation, it is hard to decide what method is currently more suited for the task of automatic acquisition of compositionality, with a slight favor for approaches based on word space model.

A takeaway message is that a pure corpus-based acquisition of graded compositionality is a hard task. While some approaches clearly outperform baselines, further advances are needed for automatic systems to be able to reproduce semantic compositionality.

Acknowledgments

We thank Emiliano Guevara for helping with the preparation of the evaluation scripts and the initial task description. This work was partially supported by the German Federal Ministry of Economics (BMWi) under the project Theseus (number 01MQ07019).

References

Colin Bannard, Timothy Baldwin, and Alex Lascarides. 2003. A statistical approach to the semantics of verb-particles. In *Proc. of the ACL-SIGLEX Workshop on Multiword Expressions: Analysis, Acquisition and Treatment*, pages 65–72, Sapporo, Japan.

Marco Baroni, Silvia Bernardini, Adriano Ferraresi, and Eros Zanchetta. 2009. The WaCky wide web: a collection of very large linguistically processed web-crawled corpora. *Language Resources and Evaluation*.

Chris Biemann and Valerie Nygaard. 2010. Crowdsourcing WordNet. In *Proc. of the 5th International Conference of the Global WordNet Association (GWC-2010)*, Mumbai, India.

Graham Katz and Eugenie Giesbrecht. 2006. Automatic identification of non-compositional multi-word expressions using latent semantic analysis. In *Proceedings of the ACL/COLING-06 Workshop on Multiword Expressions: Identifying and Exploiting Underlying Properties*, pages 12–19, Sydney, Australia.

Ivan A. Sag, Timothy Baldwin, Francis Bond, Ann Copestake, and Dan Flickinger. 2002. Multiword Expressions: A Pain in the Neck for NLP. In *Proc. of the 3rd International Conference on Intelligent Text Processing and Computational Linguistics (CICLing-2002)*, pages 1–15, Mexico City, Mexico.

Peter D. Turney and Patrick Pantel. 2010. From Frequency to Meaning: Vector Space Models of Semantics. *Journal of Artificial Intelligence Research*, 37:141–188.

Shared task system description: Frustratingly hard compositionality prediction

Anders Johannsen, Hector Martinez Alonso, Christian Rishøj and Anders Søgaard
Center for Language Technology
University of Copenhagen
{ajohannsen|alonso|crjensen|soegaard}@hum.ku.dk

Abstract

We considered a wide range of features for the DiSCo 2011 shared task about compositionality prediction for word pairs, including COALS-based endocentricity scores, compositionality scores based on distributional clusters, statistics about wordnet-induced paraphrases, hyphenation, and the likelihood of long translation equivalents in other languages. Many of the features we considered correlated significantly with human compositionality scores, but in support vector regression experiments we obtained the best results using only COALS-based endocentricity scores. Our system was nevertheless the best performing system in the shared task, and average error reductions over a simple baseline in cross-validation were 13.7% for English and 50.1% for German.

1 Introduction

The challenge in the DiSCo 2011 shared task is to estimate and predict the semantic compositionality of word pairs. Specifically, the data set consists of adjective-noun, subject-verb and object-verb pairs in English and German. The organizers also provided the Wacky corpora for English and German with lowercased lemmas.[1] In addition, we also experimented with wordnets and using Europarl corpora for the two languages (Koehn, 2005), but none of the features based on these resources were used in the final submission.

Semantic compositionality is an ambiguous term in the linguistics litterature. It may refer to the position that the meaning of sentences is built from the meaning of its parts through very general principles of application, as for example in type-logical grammars. It may also just refer to a typically not very well defined measure of semantic transparency of expressions or syntactic constructions, best illustrated by examples:

(1) pull the plug

(2) educate people

The verb-object word pair in example (1) is in the training data rated as much less compositional than example (2). The intuition is that the meaning of the whole is less related to the meaning of the parts. The compositionality relation is not defined more precisely, however, and this may in part explain why compositionality prediction seems frustratingly hard.

2 Features

Many of our features were evaluated with different amounts of *slop*. The slop parameter permits non-exact matches without resorting to language-specific shallow patterns. The words in the compounds are allowed to move around in the sentence one position at a time. The value of the parameter is the maximum number of steps. Set to zero, it is equivalent to an exact match. Below are a couple of example configurations. Note that in order for w_1 and w_2 to swap positions, we must have slop > 1 since slop=1 would place them on top of each other.

$x\ x\ w_1\ w_2\ x\ x$ (slop=0)
$x\ x\ w_1\ x\ w_2\ x$ (slop=1)
$x\ x\ w_1\ x\ x\ w_2$ (slop=2)
$x\ x\ w_2\ w_1\ x\ x$ (slop=2)

[1] http://wacky.sslmit.unibo.it/

Proceedings of the Workshop on Distributional Semantics and Compositionality (DiSCo'2011), pages 29–32,
Portland, Oregon, 24 June 2011.

2.1 LEFT-ENDOC, RIGHT-ENDOC and DISTR-DIFF

These features measure the endocentricity of a word pair w_1 w_2. The distribution of w_1 is likely to be similar to the distribution of "w_1 w_2" if w_1 is the syntactic head of "w_1 w_2". The same is to be expected for w_2, when w_2 is the head.

Syntactic endocentricity is related to compositionality, but the implication is one-way only. A highly compositional compound is endocentric, but an endocentric compound need not be highly compositional. For example, the distribution of "olive oil", which is endocentric and highly compositional, is very similar to the distribution of "oil", the head word. On the other hand, "golden age" which is ranked as highly *non-compositional* in the training data, is certainly endocentric. The distribution of "golden age" is not very different from that of "age".

We used COALS (Rohde et al., 2009) to calculate word distributions. The COALS algorithm builds a word-to-word semantic space from a corpus. We used the implementation by Jurgens and Stevens (2010), generating the semantic space from the Wacky corpora for English and German with duplicate sentences removed and low-frequency words substituted by dummy symbols. The word pairs have been fed to COALS as compounds that have to be treated as single tokens, and the semantic space has been generated and reduced using singular value decompositon. The vectors for w_1, w_2 and "w_1 w_2" are calculated, and we compute the cosine distance between the semantic space vectors for the word pair and its parts, and between the parts themselves, namely for "w_1 w_2" and w_1, for "w_1 w_2" and w_2, and for w_1 and w_2, say for "olive oil" and "olive", for "olive oil" and "oil", and for "olive" and "oil". LEFT-ENDOC is the cosine distance between the left word and the compound. RIGHT-ENDOC is the cosine distance between the right word and the compound. Finally, DISTR-DIFF is the cosine distance between the two words, w_1 and w_2.

2.2 BR-COMP

To accommodate for the weaknesses of syntactic endocentricity features, we also tried introducing compositionality scores based on hierarchical distributional clusters that would model semantic compositionality more directly. The scores are referred to below as BR-COMP (compositionality scores based on Brown clusters), and the intuition behind these scores is that a word pair "w_1 w_2", e.g. "hot dog", is non-compositional if w_1 and w_2 have high collocational strength, but if w_1 is replaced with a different word w_1' with similar distribution, e.g. "warm", then "w_1' w_2" is less collocational. Similarly, if w_2 is replaced with a different word w_2' with similar distribution, e.g. "terrier", then "w_1 w_2'" is also much less collocational than "w_1 w_2".

We first induce a hierarchical clustering of the words in the Wacky corpora $cl : W \rightarrow 2^W$ with W the set of words in our corpora, using publicly available software.[2] Let the collocational strength of the two words w_1 and w_2 be $G^2(w_1, w_2)$. We then compute the average collocational strength of distributional clusters, BR-CS (collocational strength of Brown clusters):

$$\text{BR-CS}(w_1, w_2) = \frac{\Sigma^N_{x \in cl(w_1), x' \in cl(w_2)} G^2(x, x')}{N}$$

with $N = |cl(w_1)| \times |cl(w_2)|$. We now let $\text{BR-COMP}(w_1, w_2) = \frac{\text{BR-CS}(w_1,w_2)}{G^2(w_1,w_2)}$.

The Brown clusters were built with $C = 1000$ and a cut-off frequency of 1000. With these settings the number of word types per cluster is quite high, which of course has a detrimental effect on the semantic coherence of the cluster. To counter this we choose to restrict $cl(w)$ and $cl(w')$ to include only the 50 most frequently occurring terms.

2.3 PARAPHR

These features have to do with alternative phrasings using synonyms from Princeton WordNet [3] and GermaNet[4]. One word in the compound is held constant while the other is replaced with its synonyms. The intuition is again that non-compositional compounds are much more frequent than any compound that results from replacing one of the constituent words with one of its synonyms. For "hot dog" we thus generate "hot terrier" and "warm dog", but not "warm terrier". Specifically, $\text{PARAPHR}_{\geq 100}$ means

[2]http://www.cs.berkeley.edu/~pliang/software/

[3]http://wordnet.princeton.edu/

[4]GermaNet Copyright © 1996, 2008 by University of Tübingen.

that at least one of the alternative compounds has a document count of more than 100 in the corpus. PARAPHR$_{av}$ is the average count for all paraphrases, PARAPHR$_{sum}$ is the sum of these counts, and PARAPHR$_{rel}$ is the average count for all paraphrases over the count of the word pair in question.

2.4 HYPH

The HYPH features were inspired by Bergsma et al. (2010). It was only used for English. Specifically, we used the relative frequency of hyphenated forms as features. For adjective-noun pairs we counted the number of hyphenated occurrences, e.g. "front-page", and divided that number by the number of non-hyphenated occurrences, e.g. "front page". For subject-verb and object-verb pairs, we add *-ing* to the verb, e.g. "information-collecting", and divided the number of such forms with non-hyphenated equivalents, e.g. "information collecting".

2.5 TRANS-LEN

The intuition behind our bilingual features is that non-compositional words typically translate into a single word or must be paraphrased using multiple words (circumlocution or periphrasis). TRANS-LEN is the probability that the phrase's translation, possibly with intervening articles and markers, is longer than l_{min} and shorter than l_{max}, i.e.:

$$\text{TRANS-LEN}(w_1, w_2, l_{min}, l_{max}) = \frac{\Sigma_{\tau \in trans(w_1\ w_2), l_1 \leq |\tau| \leq l_2} P(\sigma | w_1\ w_2)}{\Sigma_{\tau \in trans(w_1\ w_2)} P(\sigma | w_1\ w_2)}$$

We use English and German Europarl (Koehn, 2005) to train our translation models. In particular, we use the phrase tables of the Moses PB-SMT system[5] trained on a lemmatized version of the WMT11 parallel corpora for English and German. Below TRANS-LEN-n will be the probability of the translation of a word pair being n or more words. We also experimented with average translation length as a feature, but this did not correlate well with semantic compositionality.

[5]http://statmt.org

feat	ρ English	German
rel-type = ADJ_NN	0.0750	*0.1711
rel-type = V_SUBJ	0.0151	**0.2883
rel-type = V_OBJ	0.0880	0.0825
LEFT-ENDOC	**0.3257	*0.1637
RIGHT-ENDOC	**0.3896	0.1379
DISTR-DIFF	*0.1885	0.1128
HYPH (5)	0.1367	-
HYPH (5) reversed	*0.1829	-
G^2	0.1155	0.0535
BR-CS	*0.1592	0.0242
BR-COMP	0.0292	0.0024
Count (5)	0.0795	*0.1523
PARAPHR$_{\geq \lvert w_1\ w-2 \rvert}$	0.1123	0.1242
PARAPHR$_{rel}$ (5)	0.0906	0.0013
PARAPHR$_{av}$ (1)	0.1080	0.0743
PARAPHR$_{av}$ (5)	0.1313	0.0707
PARAPHR$_{sum}$ (1)	0.0496	0.0225
PARAPHR$_{\geq 100}$ (1)	**0.2434	0.0050
PARAPHR$_{\geq 100}$ (5)	**0.2277	0.0198
TRANS-LEN-1	0.0797	0.0509
TRANS-LEN-2	0.1109	0.0158
TRANS-LEN-3	0.0935	0.0489
TRANS-LEN-5	0.0240	0.0632

Figure 1: Correlations. Coefficients marked with * are significant ($p < 0.05$), and coefficients marked with ** are highly significant ($p < 0.01$). We omit features with different slop values if they perform significantly worse than similar features.

3 Correlations

We have introduced five different kinds of features, four of which are supposed to model semantic compositionality directly. For feature selection, we therefore compute the correlation of features with compositionality scores and select features that correlate significantly with compositionality. The features are then used for regression experiments.

4 Regression experiments

For our regression experiments, we use support vector regression with a high (7) degree kernel. Otherwise we use default parameters of publicly available software.[6] In our experiments, however, we were not able to produce substantially better results than what can be obtained using only the features LEFT-ENDOC and RIGHT-ENDOC. In fact, for German using only LEFT-ENDOC gave slightly better results than using both. These features are also those that correlate best with human compositionality scores according to Figure 1. Consequently, we only use

[6]http://www.csie.ntu.edu.tw/~cjlin/libsvm/

these features in our official runs. Our evaluations below are cross-validation results on training and development data using leave-one-out. We compare using only LEFT-ENDOC and RIGHT-ENDOC (for English) with using all significant features that seem relatively independent. For English, we used LEFT-ENDOC, RIGHT-ENDOC, DISTR-DIFF, HYPH (5) reversed, BR-CS, PARAPHR$_{\geq}$100 (1). For German, we used rel-type = ADJ_NN, rel-type=V_SUBJ and RIGHT-ENDOC. We only optimized on numeric scores. The submitted coarse-grained scores were obtained using average +/- average deviation.[7]

	English		German	
	dev	test	dev	test
BL	18.395		47.123	
all sign. indep.	19.22		**23.02**	
L-END+R-END	**15.89**	16.19	23.51	24.03
err.red (L+R)	0.137		0.501	

5 Discussion

Our experiments have shown that the DiSCo 2011 shared task about compositionality prediction was a tough challenge. This may be because of the fine-grained compositionality metric or because of inconsistencies in annotation, but note also that the syntactically oriented features seem to perform a lot better than those trying to single out semantic compositionality from syntactic endocentricity and collocational strength. For example, LEFT-ENDOC, RIGHT-ENDOC and BR-CS correlate with compositionality scores, whereas BR-COMP does not, although it is supposed to model compositionality more directly. Could it perhaps be that annotations reflect syntactic endocentricity or distributional similarity to a high degree, rather than what is typically thought of as semantic compositionality?

Consider a couple of examples of adjective-noun pairs in English in Figure 2 for illustration. These examples are taken from the training data, but we have added our subjective judgments about semantic and syntactic markedness and collocational strength (peaking at G^2 scores). It seems that semantic markedness is less important for scores than syntactic markedness and collocational strength. In particular, the combination of syntactic markedness and collocational strength makes annotators rank word pairs such as *happy birthday* and *open source* as non-compositional, although they seem to be fully compositional from a semantic perspective. This may explain why our COALS-features are so predictive of human compositionality scores, and why G^2 correlates better with these scores than BR-COMP.

	sem	**syn**	**coll**	**score**
floppy disk			✓	61
free kick	✓			77
happy birthday		✓	✓	47
large scale		✓	✓	55
old school	✓	✓	✓	37
open source		✓	✓	49
real life		✓		69
small group				91

Figure 2: Subjective judgments about semantic and syntactic markedness and collocational strength.

6 Conclusions

In our experiments for the DiSCo 2011 shared task we have considered a wide range of features and showed that some of them correlate significantly and sometimes highly significantly with human compositionality scores. In our regression experiments, however, our best results were obtained with only one or two COALS-based endocentricity features. We report error reductions of 13.7% for English and 50.1% for German.

[7]These thresholds were poorly chosen, by the way. Had we chosen less balanced cut-offs, say 0 and 72, our improved accuracy on coarse-grained scores (59.4) would have been comparable to and slightly better than the best submitted coarse-grained scores (58.5).

References

Shane Bergsma, Aditya Bhargava, Hua He, and Grzegorz Kondrak. 2010. Predicting the semantic compositionality of prefix verbs. In *EMNLP*.

David Jurgens and Keith Stevens. 2010. The S-Space package: an open source package for word space models. In *ACL*.

Philipp Koehn. 2005. Europarl: a parallel corpus for statistical machine translation. In *MT-Summit*.

Douglas Rohde, Laura Gonnerman, and David Plaut. 2009. An improved model of semantic similarity based on lexical co-occurrence. In *Cognitive Science*.

Identifying Collocations to Measure Compositionality : Shared Task System Description

Ted Pedersen
Department of Computer Science
University of Minnesota
Duluth, MN 55812 USA
tpederse@d.umn.edu

Abstract

This paper describes three systems from the University of Minnesota, Duluth that participated in the DiSCo 2011 shared task that evaluated distributional methods of measuring semantic compositionality. All three systems approached this as a problem of collocation identification, where strong collocates are assumed to be minimally compositional. duluth-1 relies on the t-score, whereas duluth-2 and duluth-3 rely on Pointwise Mutual Information (pmi). duluth-1 was the *top ranked system overall* in coarse–grained scoring, which was a 3-way category assignment where pairs were assigned values of high, medium, or low compositionality.

1 Introduction

An ngram or phrase that means more than the sum of its parts is said to be non-compositional. Well known examples include *kick the bucket* (i.e., to die) and *red tape* (i.e., bureaucratic steps). The ability to measure the degree of semantic compositionality in a unit of text is a key capability of NLP systems, since non-compositional phrases can be treated as a single unit, rather than as a series of individual words. This has a tremendous impact on word sense disambiguation systems, for example, since a non-compositional phrase will often have just one possible sense and thereby be reduced to a trivial case, whereas the combination of possible sense assignments for the words that make up a phrase can grow exponentially.

Identifying collocations is another key capability of NLP systems. Collocations are generally considered to be units of text that occur with some regularity and may have some non-compositional meaning. The Duluth systems that participated in the DiSCo 2011 shared task (Biemann and Giesbrecht, 2011) seek to determine the degree to which collocation identification techniques can be used to measure semantic compositionality. In particular, these systems are based on the following hypothesis:

> An ngram that has a high score according to a measure of association (for identifying collocations) will be less compositional (and less literal) than those that have lower scores.

The intuition underlying this hypothesis is a high score from a measure of association shows that the words in the ngram are occurring together more often than would be expected by chance, and that a non-compositional phrase is unlikely to occur in such a way that it looks like a chance event.

2 System Development

The Duluth systems were developed by identifying collocations based on frequency counts obtained from the WaCky English corpus (Baroni et al., 2009), hereafter referred to as *the corpus*. The part of speech tags were removed from the corpus, and the text was converted to lower case. A set of 139 training pairs was provided by the task organizers that had been manually rated for compositionality. This gold standard data was used to select which measures of association would form the basis of the Duluth systems. Thereafter a separate set of 174 test pairs were provided by the organizers for evaluation.

Proceedings of the Workshop on Distributional Semantics and Compositionality (DiSCo'2011), pages 33–37,
Portland, Oregon, 24 June 2011. ©2011 Association for Computational Linguistics

2.1 Collocation Discovery

The Ngram Statistics Package (Text::NSP) (Banerjee and Pedersen, 2003) was used to measure the association between the training pairs based on frequency count data collected from the corpus. All thirteen measures in the Ngram Statistics Package were employed, including the Log-likelihood Ratio (ll) (Dunning, 1993), Pointwise Mutual Information (pmi) (Church and Hanks, 1990), Mutual Information (tmi) (Church and Hanks, 1990), Poisson-Stirling (ps) (Church, 2000), Fisher's Exact Test (leftFisher, rightFisher, and twotailed) (Pedersen et al., 1996), Jaccard Coefficient (jaccard), Dice Coefficient (dice), Phi Coefficient (phi), t-score (tscore) (Church and Hanks, 1990), Pearson's Chi-Squared Test (x2), and the Odds Ratio (odds).

These measure the co-occurrence of word pairs (bigrams) relative to their individual frequencies and assess how likely it is that the word pair is occurring together by chance (and is therefore likely compositional) or has some significant pattern of occurrence as a pair (in which case it is non-compositional). More formally, many of these methods compare the observed empirical data with a model that casts the words in the bigram as independent statistical events. The measures determine the degree to which the observed data deviates from what would be expected under the model of independence. If the observed data differs significantly from that, then there is no evidence to support the hypothesis that the bigram is a chance event, and we assume that there is some interesting or significant pattern that implies non-compositionality. In some cases the training and test pairs are not adjacent (e.g., *reinvent wheel* for *reinvent the wheel*), and so window sizes of 2, 4, and 10 words were used when measuring the association between pairs of words. This means that 0, 2 and 8 intervening words were allowed, respectively.

Frequency count data for the word pairs are tabulated as shown in the example in Figure 1. The variable W_1 represents the presence or absence of **red** in the first position of each word pair, and W_2 represents the presence or absence of **tape** in the second position. This table tells us, for example, that *red tape* occurs 5,363 times (n_{11}), that *red* occurs 18,493 times (n_{1+}), and that bigrams that contain neither *red* nor *tape* occur 68,824,813 times (n_{22}). The total number of bigrams found in the corpus is 68,845,263 (n_{++}). Note that these counts are based on a window size of 2. Counts increase with a larger window size. If the window size were 10, then n_{11} would tell us how many times *red* and *tape* occurred within 8 words of each other (in order).

		W_2		
		tape	¬tape	totals
W_1	red	n_{11}= 5,363	n_{12}= 13,130	n_{1+}= 18,493
	¬red	n_{21}= 1,957	n_{22}= 68,824,813	n_{2+}= 68,826,770
	totals	n_{+1}= 7,320	n_{+2}= 68,837,943	n_{++}= 68,845,263

Figure 1: Contingency Table Counts

2.2 Scoring Word Pairs

The training pairs were ranked according to each of the measures in Text::NSP, where high scores indicate that two words (w_1 and w_2) are not occurring together by chance, and that there is a non-compositional meaning. However, high scores in the shared task meant exactly the opposite; that a word pair was highly compositional (and literal). In addition, the fine grained scoring in the shared task was on a scale of 0 to 100, and it was required that participating systems use that same scale. Thus, the scores from the measures were converted to this scale as follows:

Let the maximum value of the Text::NSP measure for all the pairs in the set under consideration be $max(m(W_1, W_2))$, where m represents the specific measure being used. Then the score for each word pair is normalized by dividing it by this maximum value, and subtracted from 1 and then multiplied by 100. More generally, the fine grained score for any word pair (w_1, w_2) as computed by a specific duluth-x system is $dx(w_1, w_2)$ and is calculated as follows:

$$dx(w_1, w_2) = 100 * (1 - \frac{m(w_1, w_2)}{max(m(W_1, W_2))}) \quad (1)$$

Coarse grained scoring is automatically performed by binning all of the resulting scores in the range 0-33 to *low*, 34 - 66 to *medium* and 67 - 100 to *high*.

Table 1: Text::NSP Rank Correlation with Gold Standard - duluth-1 corresponds to t-score window 10, duluth-2 with pmi window 10 and duluth-3 with pmi window 2

	Window Size		
Measure	2	4	10
tscore	0.1484	0.2114	**0.2674**
tmi	0.1335	0.1908	0.2361
ll	0.1336	0.1913	0.2358
frequency	0.1865	0.2100	0.2126
ps	0.0992	0.1554	0.1874
x2	0.1157	0.1172	0.1654
phi	0.1157	0.1167	0.1646
jaccard	0.1253	0.1255	0.1602
dice	0.1253	0.1255	0.1602
odds	0.0216	0.0060	0.0257
pmi	**-0.0241**	-0.0145	**0.0143**
rightFisher	-0.1768	-0.0817	0.0740
leftFisher	0.1316	0.0686	-0.0870
twotailed	-0.1445	-0.0651	-0.1064

Table 2: Text::NSP Rank Correlation with Frequency - duluth-1 corresponds to t-score window 10, duluth-2 with pmi window 10 and duluth-3 with pmi window 2

	Window Size		
Measure	2	4	10
tscore	0.9857	0.9578	**0.8477**
ps	0.8856	0.8423	0.8299
ll	0.9082	0.8459	0.6953
tmi	0.9080	0.8459	0.6951
jaccard	0.7170	0.6128	0.5527
dice	0.7170	0.6128	0.5527
phi	0.7038	0.5743	0.4308
x2	0.7039	0.5744	0.4303
rightFisher	-0.5998	-0.3279	0.2004
odds	0.3714	0.1483	-0.0353
pmi	**0.2487**	0.0789	**-0.1390**
leftFisher	0.5675	0.3500	-0.1726
twotailed	-0.5965	-0.4434	-0.2712

2.3 Correlation of Word Pairs

Before the evaluation period, it was decided that duluth-1 (our flagship system) would be based on the measure of association that had the highest Spearman's rank correlation with the fine grained gold standard annotations of the training pairs. As can be seen from Table 1, that measure was the t-score based on a window size of 10.

As an additional experiment, the ranking of the training pairs according to each measure in Text::NSP was compared to the frequency ranking in the corpus. As can be seen in Table 2, once again it was the t-score that had the highest correlation.

While the correlation with the training pairs by the t-score was encouraging, the correlation with frequency was something of a surprise, and in fact caused some concern. Could a measure that correlated so highly with frequency really be successful in measuring semantic compositionality? However, upon reflection it seemed that correlation with frequency might be quite desirable, and led to the formulation of a second hypothesis:

> Very frequent word pairs are more likely to be compositional (i.e., highly literal) than are less frequent word pairs.

The assumption that underlies this hypothesis is that the most frequent word pairs tend to be very literal and non-compositional (e.g., *for the*, *in that*) and it would (in general) be a surprise to expect a compositional pair (e.g., *above board*, *rip saw*) to attain as high a frequency.

3 duluth-1 (t-score in a 10 word window)

The duluth-1 system is based on the t-score in a 10 word window, and was selected because of its high correlation to the gold standard annotations of the training pairs and to the frequency ranking of the training pairs. The t-score optimizes both of our previous hypotheses, which suggests it should be a good choice for measuring compositionality.

By way of background, the t-score (t) is formulated as follows (Church et al., 1991), using the notation introduced in Figure 1 :

$$t = \frac{n_{11} - m_{11}}{\sqrt{n_{11}}} \qquad (2)$$

where n_{11} is the observed count of the word pair, and m_{11} is the expected value based on the hypothesized model of independence between variables W_1 and W_2. As such,

$$m_{11} = \frac{n_{1+} * n_{+1}}{n_{++}} \qquad (3)$$

If there is little difference between the observed and expected values, then the t-score is closer to zero (or even less than zero) and the pair of words can be judged to occur together simply by chance (i.e., the hypothesis of independence is true).

The t-scores for the test pairs were converted following equation (1), and then submitted for evaluation. duluth-1 placed in the middle ranks in the fine grain evaluation according to mean distance, and was the top ranked system according to the label precision evaluation of coarse grained scoring.

4 duluth-2 (pmi with window size of 10)

In studying Tables 1 and 2, it's clear that Pointwise Mutual Information (pmi) deviates rather significantly from frequency and the t-score. At the time of the evaluation, we did not know if our hypotheses that motivated the use of the t-score would prove to be true. If they did not, it seemed sensible to include the most opposite measure to the t-score, as a kind of fail safe mechanism for our systems overall. In addition, pmi has a fairly significant history of use in identifying collocations and features for other NLP tasks (e.g., (Pantel and Lin, 2002)), and so it seemed like a credible candidate.

pmi has a well known bias towards identifying words that only occur together, and tends to prefer less frequent word pairs, and this is why it diverges so significantly from the t-score and frequency. Interestingly, pmi is also based on the same observed and expected values n_{11} and m_{11} as used in the t-score (and many of the other measures), and is calculated as follows:

$$pmi = log\frac{n_{11}}{m_{11}} \tag{4}$$

If there is little difference between the observed and expected values, then pmi tends towards 0 and we treat the word pairs as independent and compositional.

duluth-2 relies on a window size of 10, since it diverges dramatically from the t-score and frequency.

5 duluth-3 (pmi with window size of 2)

duluth-3 is a very close relative of duluth-2, and differs only in that it requires word pairs to be adjacent. Given the wider window sizes in duluth-2, it is clear that if a pair has a high pmi score, they must only occur (mostly) together. duluth-3 only considers adjacent words, and so the words that make up the pairs may also appear elsewhere in the corpus. As such duluth-3 may tend to assign higher pmi scores than the more exacting duluth-2 (where high scores mean low compositionality). And in fact this is what occurred. In the coarse scoring scheme, duluth-1 only identified 2 low compositional word pairs, whereas duluth-2 identified 46 and duluth-3 identified 70.

Despite the difference in the window size the rank correlation between duluth-2 and duluth-3 is relatively high (.9330). Both performed comparably in the evaluation, being near the bottom of both the fine and coarse grained evaluations. By comparison, duluth-1 and duluth-2 have a relatively low rank correlation of .1756, and duluth-1 and duluth-3 have a modest correlation of .3438.

6 Conclusions

The Duluth systems seek to evaluate the degree to which measures of collocation are able to measure semantic compositionality as well. The results of this shared task suggest that the t-score is well suited to make coarse grained distinctions between high, medium, and low levels of compositionality, since duluth-1 was the top ranked system in the coarse grained evaluation. While this success might be considered surprising due to the simplicity of the approach, it should not be underestimated. There are two separate hypotheses that underly the t-score and its use in measuring semantic compositionality. These hold that word pairs with high measures of association are more likely to be non–compositional, and that more frequent word pairs are more likely to be compositional. Of the measures evaluated in this study, the t-score was best able to optimize both of these conditions.

7 Acknowledgements

The experiments in this paper were conducted with version 1.23 of the Ngram Statistics Package (Text::NSP), which is implemented in Perl and freely available from http://ngram.sourceforge.net.

References

S. Banerjee and T. Pedersen. 2003. The design, implementation, and use of the Ngram Statistics Package. In *Proceedings of the Fourth International Conference on Intelligent Text Processing and Computational Linguistics*, pages 370–381, Mexico City, February.

M. Baroni, S. Bernardini, A. Ferraresi, and E. Zanchetta. 2009. The WaCky wide web: A collection of very large linguistically processed web-crawled corpora. *Language Resources and Evaluation*, 43(3):209–226.

C. Biemann and E. Giesbrecht. 2011. Distributional semantics and compositionality 2011: Shared task description and results. In *Proceedings of DiSCo–2011 in conjunction ACL HLT 2011*, Portland, Oregon, June. Association for Computational Linguistics.

K. Church and P. Hanks. 1990. Word association norms, mutual information and lexicography. In *Proceedings of the 28th Annual Meeting of the Association for Computational Linguistics*, pages 76–83.

K. Church, W. Gale, P. Hanks, and D. Hindle. 1991. Using statistics in lexical analysis. In U. Zernik, editor, *Lexical Acquisition: Exploiting On-Line Resources to Build a Lexicon*. Lawrence Erlbaum Associates, Hillsdale, NJ.

K. Church. 2000. Empirical estimates of adaptation: The chance of two noriegas is closer to p/2 than p2. In *Proceedings of the 18th International Conference on Computational Linguistics (COLING-2000)*, pages 180–186, Saarbrücken, Germany.

T. Dunning. 1993. Accurate methods for the statistics of surprise and coincidence. *Computational Linguistics*, 19(1):61–74.

P. Pantel and D. Lin. 2002. Discovering word senses from text. In *Proceedings of ACM SIGKDD Conference on Knowledge Discovery and Data Mining-2002*.

T. Pedersen, M. Kayaalp, and R. Bruce. 1996. Significant lexical relationships. In *Proceedings of the Thirteenth National Conference on Artificial Intelligence*, pages 455–460, Portland, OR, August.

Shared task system description: Measuring the Compositionality of Bigrams using Statistical Methodologies

Tanmoy Chakraborty, Santanu Pal, Tapabrata Mondal, Tanik Saikh, Sivaji Bandyopadhyay
Department of Computer Science and Engineering
Jadavpur University
its_tanmoy@yahoo.co.in, santanu.pal.ju@gmail.com, tapabratamondal@gmail.com, tanik4u@gmail.com, sivaji_cse_ju@yahoo.com

Abstract

The measurement of relative compositionality of bigrams is crucial to identify Multi-word Expressions (MWEs) in Natural Language Processing (NLP) tasks. The article presents the experiments carried out as part of the participation in the shared task '*Distributional Semantics and Compositionality (DiSCo)*' organized as part of the *DiSCo* workshop in ACL-HLT 2011. The experiments deal with various collocation based statistical approaches to compute the relative compositionality of three types of bigram phrases (Adjective-Noun, Verb-subject and Verb-object combinations). The experimental results in terms of both fine-grained and coarse-grained compositionality scores have been evaluated with the human annotated gold standard data. Reasonable results have been obtained in terms of average point difference and coarse precision.

1 Introduction

The present work examines the relative compositionality of Adjective-Noun (ADJ-NN; e.g., *blue chip*), Verb-subject (V-SUBJ; where noun acting as a subject of a verb, e.g., *name imply*) and Verb-object (V-OBJ; where noun acting as an object of a verb, e.g., *beg question*) combinations using collocation based statistical approaches. Measuring the relative compositionality is useful in applications such as machine translation where the highly non-compositional collocations can be handled in a special way (Hwang and Sasaki, 2005).

Multi-word expressions (MWEs) are sequences of words that tend to co-occur more frequently than chance and are either idiosyncratic or decomposable into multiple simple words (Baldwin, 2006). Deciding idiomaticity of MWEs is highly important for machine translation, information retrieval, question answering, lexical acquisition, parsing and language generation. *Compositionality* refers to the degree to which the meaning of a MWE can be predicted by combining the meanings of its components. Unlike *syntactic compositionality* (e.g. *by and large*), *semantic compositionality* is continuous (Baldwin, 2006).

Several studies have been carried out for detecting compositionality of noun-noun MWEs using WordNet hypothesis (Baldwin et al., 2003), verb-particle constructions using statistical similarities (Bannard et al., 2003; McCarthy et al., 2003) and verb-noun pairs using Latent Semantic Analysis (Katz and Giesbrecht, 2006).

Our contributions are two-fold: firstly, we experimentally show that collocation based statistical compositionality measurement can assist in identifying the continuum of compositionality of MWEs. Secondly, we show that supervised weighted parameter tuning results in accuracy that is comparable to the best manually selected combination of parameters.

Proceedings of the Workshop on Distributional Semantics and Compositionality (DiSCo'2011), pages 38–42,
Portland, Oregon, 24 June 2011.

2 Proposed Methodologies

The present task was to identify the numerical judgment of compositionality of individual phrase. The statistical co-occurrence features used in this experiment are described.

Frequency: If two words occur together quite frequently, the lexical meaning of the composition may be different from the combination of their individual meanings. The frequency of an individual phrase is directly used in the following methods.

Point-wise Information (PMI): An information-theoretic motivated measure for discovering interesting collocations is *point-wise mutual information* (Church and Hanks, 1990). It is originally defined as the mutual information between particular events *X* and *Y* and in our case the occurrence of particular words, as follows:

$$PMI(x\ y) = \log_2 \frac{P(x,y)}{P(x).P(y)} \approx \log_2 \frac{NC(x,y)}{C(x).C(y)} \quad (1)$$

PMI represents the amount of information provided by the occurrence of the event represented by *X* about the occurrence of the event represented by *Y*.

T-test: T-test has been widely used for collocation discovery. This statistical test tells us the probability of a certain constellation (Nugues, 2006). It looks at the mean and variance of a sample of measurements. The null hypothesis is that the sample is drawn from a distribution with mean. T-score is computed using the equation (2):

$$t(x,y) = \frac{mean(P(X,Y)) - mean\ (P(X))mean(P(Y))}{\sqrt{(\sigma^2 P(X,Y)) + \sigma^2(P(X))\sigma^2\ (P(Y))}}$$

$$\approx \frac{C(X,Y) - \frac{C(X)C(Y)}{N}}{\sqrt{C(X,Y)}} \dots\dots\dots\dots\dots\dots (2)$$

In both the equations (1) and(2), *C(x)* and *C(y)* are respectively the frequencies of word *X* and word *Y* in the corpus, *C(X,Y)* is the combined frequency of the bigrams <X Y> and N is the total number of tokens in the corpus. Mean value of *P(X,Y)* represents the average probability of the bigrams <X Y>. The bigram count can be extended to the frequency of word X when it is followed or preceded by Y in the window of K words (here K=1).

Perplexity: Perplexity is defined as $2^{H(X)}$

$$2^{H(X)} = 2^{-\sum_x P(x)\log_2 P(x)} \dots\dots\dots\dots (3)$$

where *H(X)* is the cross-entropy of *X*. Here, *X* is the candidate bigram whose value is measured throughout the corpus. Perplexity is interpreted as the average "branching factor" of a word: the statistically weighted number of words that follow a given word. As we see from equation (4), Perplexity is equivalent to entropy. The only advantage of perplexity is that it results in numbers more comprehensible for human beings. Here, perplexity is measured at both root level and surface level.

Chi-square test: The t-test assumes that probabilities are approximately normally distributed, which may not be true in general (Manning and Schütze, 2003). An alternative test for dependence which does not assume normally distributed probabilities is the χ^2-test (pronounced "chi-square test"). In the simplest case, this test is applied to a 2-by-2 table as shown below:

	X = *new*	X ≠ *new*
Y= *companies*	n_{11} (*new companies*)	n_{12} (e.g., *old companies*)
Y ≠ *companies*	n_{21} (e.g., *new machines*)	n_{22} (e.g., *old machines*)

Table 1: A 2-by-2 table showing the dependence of occurrences of *new* and *companies*

Each variable in the above table depicts its individual frequency, e.g., n_{11} denotes the frequency of the phrase "new companies".

The idea is to compare the observed frequencies in the table with the expected frequencies when the words occur independently. If the difference between observed and expected frequencies is large, then we can reject the null hypothesis of independence. The equation for this test is defined below:

$$\chi^2 = \frac{N(O_{11}O_{22} - O_{12}O_{21})^2}{(O_{11}+O_{12})(O_{11}+O_{21})(O_{12}+O_{22})(O_{21}+O_{22})} \quad (4)$$

$$\text{where } O_{ij} = \frac{\sum_k n_{ik}}{N} \times \frac{\sum_k n_{kj}}{N} \times N$$

N is the number of tokens in the corpus.

3 Used Corpora and Dataset

The system has used the **WaCkypedia_EN**[1] **corpora which are** a 2009 dump of the English Wikipedia (about 800 million tokens). The corpus was POS-tagged and lemmatized followed by full dependency parsing. The total number of candidate items for each relation type extracted from the corpora is: ADJ-NN (144, 102), V-SUBJ (74, 56), V-OBJ (133, 96). The first number within brackets is the number of items with fine-grained score, while the second number refers to the number of items with coarse grained score. These candidate phrases are split into 40% training, 10% validation and 50% test sets. The training data set consists of three columns: relation (e.g., EN_V_OBJ), phrase (e.g., *provide evidence*) and judgment score (e.g. "38" or "high"). Scores were averaged over valid judgments per phrase and normalized between 0 and 100. These numerical scores are used for the Average Point Difference score. For coarse-grained score, phrases with numerical judgments between 0 and 33 as "low", 34 to 66 as "medium" and 66 and over got the label "high".

4 System Architecture

The candidate items for each relation type are put in a database. For each candidate, all the statistical co-occurrence feature values like frequency, PMI, T-test, Perplexity (root and surface levels) and Chi-square tests are calculated. The final fine-grained scores are computed as the simple average and weighted average of the individual statistical co-occurrence scores. Another fine-grained score is based on the T-test score that performed best on the training data. Coarse-grained scores are obtained for all the three fine-grained scores.

5 Weighted Combination

The validation data is used as the development data set for our system. The weighted average of the individual statistical co-occurrence scores is calculated by assigning different weights to each co-occurrence feature score. The weights are calculated from the training data using the average point difference error associated with the co-occurrence feature. The feature which gives minimum error score is assigned the higher weight. For each co-occurrence feature score i, if the error on the training data is e_i, the weight W_i assigned to the co-occurrence feature score i is defined as:

$$W_i = \frac{100 - e_i}{\sum_i (100 - e_i)} \qquad (5)$$

The individual co-occurrence feature scores are normalized to be in the range of 0 to 1 before calculating the weighted sum.

Note that, when measuring coarse-precision, the fine-grained scores are bucketed into three bins as explained in Section 3.

6 Evaluation Metrics

The system output is evaluated using the following evaluation metrics:

Average Point Difference (APD): the mean error (0 to 100) is measured by computing the average difference of system score and test data score. The minimum value implies the minimum error and the maximum accuracy of the system.

Coarse Precision (CP): the test data scores are binned into three grades of compositionality (non-compositional, somewhat compositional, and fully-compositional), ordering the output by score and optimally mapping the system output to the three bins.

Errors	PMI	T test	Perx-Root	Perx-Surface	chi square	Average	Weighted Average
APD	29.35	**24.25**	35.23	31.4	36.57	**21.22**	**21.20**
CP	0.31	**0.60**	0.48	0.42	0.45	**0.57**	**0.62**

Table 2: Evaluation results on different approaches on validation data

[1] http://wacky.sslmit.unibo.it/

System	Spearman rho	Kendall's Tau	Average Point Difference (APD)				Coarse Precision (CP)			
			ALL	**ADJ-NN**	**V-SUBJ**	**V-OBJ**	**ALL**	**ADJ-NN**	**V-SUBJ**	**V-OBJ**
Baseline	0.20	0.20	32.82	34.57	29.83	32.34	0.297	0.288	0.300	0.308
RUN-1	**0.33**	**0.23**	**22.67**	**25.32**	**17.71**	**22.16**	0.441	0.442	0.462	0.425
RUN-2	0.32	0.22	22.94	25.69	17.51	22.60	0.458	0.481	0.462	0.425
RUN-3	-0.04	-0.03	25.75	30.03	26.91	19.77	**0.475**	**0.442**	**0.346**	**0.600**

Table 3: Overall System results on test set

Spearman's rho coefficient: it is used to estimate strength and direction of association between two ordinal level variables (i.e., gold standard results and system results). It can range from -1.00 to 1.00.

Kendall's tau rank coefficient: it is a measure of rank correlation, i.e., the similarity of the orderings of the gold standard results and the system results. This coefficient must be in the range from -1 (complete disagreement) to 1 (complete agreement).

7 Experimental Results

The system has been trained using the training data set with their fine-grained score. The evaluation results on the validation set are shown in Table 2. It is observed that T-test gives the best results on the validation data set in terms of precision. Based on the validation set results, three procedural approaches are run and three results are reported on the test data.

RUN-1 (Weighted Combination): These results are obtained from the weighted combination of individual scores. Both the perplexity measures are not useful to make significant gain over the compositionality measure. For the rank combination experiments, the best co-occurrence measures, i.e., PMI, Chi-square and T-test are considered. For the weighted combination, the results are reported for the weight triple (0.329, 0.309, 0.364) for PMI, Chi-square and T-test respectively.

RUN-2 (Average Combination): These results are reported by simply averaging the values obtained from the five measures.

RUN-3 (Best Scoring Measure: T-test): The T-test results are observed as the best scoring measure used in this experiment.

When calculating the coarse-grained score the compositionality of each phrase is tagged as *'high'*, *'medium'* or *'low'* discussed in Section 3.

The final test data set has been evaluated on the gold standard data developed by the organizers and the results on the three submitted runs are described in Table 3. The positive value of Spearman's rho coefficient implies that the system results are in the same direction with the gold standard results; while the Kandell's tau indicates the independence of the system value with the gold standard data. As expected, Table 3 shows that the weighted average score (Run 1) gives better accuracy for all phrases based on the APD scores. On the other hand, the T-test results (Run 3) give high accuracy for the coarse precision calculation while it is in the last position for ADP scores.

8 Conclusions

We have demonstrated the usefulness of statistical evidences to indicate the continuum of compositionality of the bigrams, i.e., adjective-noun, verb-subject and verb-object combinations. The coarse precision can be improved if three ranges of numerical values can be tuned properly and the size of the three bins can be varied significantly. As part of our future task, we plan to use other statistical collocation-based methods (e.g. Log-likelihood ratio, Relative frequency ratios etc.).

Acknowledgement

The work has been carried out with support from "Indian Language to Indian Language Machine Translation (ILMT) System Phrase II", funded by DIT, Govt. of India.

References

Young-Sook Hwang and Yutaka Sasaki. 2005. Context-dependent SMT model using bilingual verb-noun collocation. In proceedings of 43rd Annual Meeting of association for Compositional Linguistics (ACL' 05).

T. Baldwin. 2006. Compositionality and MWEs: Six of one, half a dozen of the other? In proceedings of the MWE workshop. ACL.

T. Baldwin, C. Bannard, T. Tanaka, and D. Widdows. 2003. An empirical model of MWE decomposability. In proceedings of the MWE workshop. ACL.

C. Bannard, T. Baldwin, and A. Lascarides. 2003. A statistical approach to the semantics of verb-particles. In proceedings of the MWE workshop. ACL.

G. Katz and E. Giesbrecht. 2006. Automatic identification of non-compositional MWEs using latent semantic analysis. In proceedings of the MWE workshop. ACL.

Church, K. W. and Hanks, P. 1990. Word association norms, mutual information and lexicography. Computational Linguistics, 16(1):22-29

Christopher D. Manning and Hinrich Schűtze,. 2003. Foundations of Statistical Natural Language Processing, The MIT Press, Cambridge, Massachusetts, London, England.

Pierre M. Nugues. 2006. An Introduction to Language Processing with Perl and Prolog, Springer.

Detecting compositionality using semantic vector space models based on syntactic context. Shared task system description*

Guillermo Garrido
NLP & IR Group at UNED
Madrid, Spain
ggarrido@lsi.uned.es

Anselmo Peñas
NLP & IR Group at UNED
Madrid, Spain
anselmo@lsi.uned.es

Abstract

This paper reports on the participation of the NLP GROUP at UNED in the DiSCo'2011 compositionality evaluation task. The aim of the task is to predict compositionality judgements assigned by human raters to candidate phrases, in English and German, from three common grammatical relations: adjective-noun, subject-verb and subject-object.

Our participation is restricted to adjective-noun relations in English. We explore the use of syntactic-based contexts obtained from large corpora to build classifiers that model the compositionality of the semantics of such pairs.

1 Introduction

This paper reports on the NLP GROUP at UNED 's participation in DiSCo'2011 Shared Task. We attempt to model the notion of compositionality from analyzing language use in large corpora. In doing this, we are assuming the distributional hypothesis: *words that occur in similar contexts tend to have similar meanings* (Harris, 1954). For a review of the field, see (Turney and Pantel, 2010).

1.1 Approach

In previous approaches to compositionality detection, different kinds of information have been used: morphological, lexical, syntactic, and distributional. For our participation, we are interested in exploring, exclusively, the reach of pure syntactic information to explain semantics.

Our approach draws from the Background Knowledge Base representation of texts introduced in (Peñas and Hovy, 2010). We hypothesize that behind syntactic dependencies in natural language there are semantic relations; and that syntactic contexts can be leveraged to represent meaning, particularly of nouns. A system could learn these semantic relations from large quantities of natural language text, to build an independent semantic resource, a Background Knowledge Base (BKB) (Peñas and Hovy, 2010).

From a dependency-parsed corpus, we automatically harvest meaning-bearing patterns, matching the dependency trees to a set of pre-specified syntactic patterns, similarly to (Pado and Lapata, 2007). Patterns are matched to dependency trees to produce propositions, carriers of minimal semantic units. Their frequency in the collection is the fundamental source of our representation.

Our participation, due to time constraints, is restricted to adjective-noun pairs in English.

2 System Description

Our hypothesis can be spelled out as: words (or word compounds) with similar syntactic contexts are semantically similar.

The intuition behind our approach is that non-compositional compounds are units of meaning. Then, the meaning of an adjective-noun combination that is not compositional should be different from the meaning of the noun alone; for similar

* This work has been partially supported by the Spanish Ministry of Science and Innovation, through the project Holopedia (TIN2010-21128-C02), and the Regional Government of Madrid, through the project MA2VICMR (S2009/TIC1542).

Proceedings of the Workshop on Distributional Semantics and Compositionality (DiSCo'2011), pages 43–47,
Portland, Oregon, 24 June 2011. ©2011 Association for Computational Linguistics

approaches, see (Baldwin et al., 2003; Katz and Giesbrecht, 2006; Mitchell and Lapata, 2010). We propose studying the distributional semantics of a *adjective-noun compound*; in particular, we will represent it via its syntactic contexts.

2.1 Adjective-noun compounds

Given a particular adjective-noun compound, denoted $\langle a, n \rangle$, we want to measure its compositionality by comparing its syntactic contexts to those of the noun: $\langle n \rangle$. After exploring the dataset we realized that considering nouns alone introduced noise, as contexts of the target and different meanings of the noun might be hard to separate; in order to soften this problem we decided to compare the occurrences of the $\langle a, n \rangle$ pair to those of the noun with a *different adjective*.

Given a dependency-parsed corpus C, we denote N the set of all nouns occurring in C and A the set of all adjectives. An adjective-noun pair, $\langle a, n \rangle$, is an occurrence in the dependency parse of the sentence of an arc (a, n), where n is the governor of an adjectival relation, with a as modifier. We define the *complementary* of $\langle a, n \rangle$ as the set of all adjective-noun pairs with the same noun but a different adjective:

$$\langle a^c, n \rangle = \{\langle b, n \rangle \text{ such that } b \in A, b \neq a\}$$

In order to detect compositionality, we compare the semantics of $\langle a, n \rangle$ to those of its complementary $\langle a^c, n \rangle$. We use syntactic context as the representation of these compounds' semantics.

We call *target pairs* those $\langle a, n \rangle$ in which we are interested, as they appear in the training, validation, or test sets for the task. For each of them, its complementary target is: $\langle a^c, n \rangle$.

We model the syntactic contexts of any $\langle a, n \rangle$ pair as a *set* of vectors in a set of vector spaces defined as follows. After inspection of the corpus, and its dependency parse annotation layer, we manually specified a few syntactic relations, which we consider codify the relevant syntactic relations in which an $\langle a, n \rangle$ takes part. For each of these syntactic relations, we built a vector space model, and we represented as a vector in it each of the target patterns, and each of their respective complementary targets. To compute compositionality of a target, we calculated the cosine similarity between the target vector and the target's complementary vector. So, for each syntactic relation, and for each target, we have a value of its similarity to the complementary target. These similarity values are considered features, from which to learn the compositionality of targets.

For results comparability, we used the PukWaC corpus[1] as dataset. PukWaC adds to UkWaC a layer of syntactic dependency annotation. The corpus has been POS-tagged and lemmatized with the TreeTagger[2]. The dependency parse was done with MaltParser (Nivre and Scholz, 2004).

2.2 Implementation details

We defined a set of 19 syntactic patterns that define interesting relations in which an $\langle a, n \rangle$ pair might take part, trying to exploit the dependencies produced by the MaltParser (Nivre and Scholz, 2004), including:

- Relations to a verb, other than the auxiliary to be and to have: subject; object; indirect object; subject of a passive construction; logical subject of a passive construction.
- The relations defined in the previous point, enriched with a noun that acts as the other element of a [subject-verb-object] or [subject-passive verb-logical subject] construction.
- Collapsed prepositional complexes.
- Noun complexes.
- As subject or object of the verb to be.
- Modified by a second adjective.
- As modifier of a possessive.

The paths were defined manually to match our intuitions of which are the paths that best describe the context of an $\langle a, n \rangle$pair, similarly to (Pado and Lapata, 2007). For each of the patterns, the set of words that are related through it to the target $\langle a, n \rangle$ define the target's *context*.

For most of our processing, we used simple programs implemented in Prolog and Python. We implemented Prolog programs to model the dependency parsed sentences of the full PUkWaC corpus, and to match and extract these patterns from them. After an aggregating step, where proper nouns, numbers and dates are substituted by place-holder vari-

[1] Available at `http://wacky.sslmit.unibo.it`

[2] `http://www.ims.uni-stuttgart.de/projekte/corplex/TreeTagger/DecisionTreeTagger.html`

ables, they amount to over 16 million instances, representing the syntactic relations in which every $\langle a, n \rangle$ pair in the corpus takes part. In further processing, only those that affect the target pairs, or the nouns in them, have to be taken into account.

As described above, each pattern we have defined yields a vector space, where each target and its complementary are represented as a vector. The base vectors of the vector space model for a pattern are the words that are syntactic contexts, with that syntactic pattern, of any target in the target set[3].

The value of the coordinate for a target and a base vector is the frequency of the context word as related to the target by the pattern. All frequencies were locally scaled using logarithms[4].

For each syntactic pattern, and for each target and complementary, we have two vectors, representing their meanings in the vector space distributional model. The complementary vector, in particular, represents the centroid (average) of the meanings of all $\langle b, n \rangle$ pairs, that share the noun with the target but have a different adjective, b

We propose that a target will be more compositional if its meaning is more similar to the meaning of the centroid of its complementary, that codifies the general meaning of that noun (whenever it appears with a different adjective).

For each syntactic pattern and target, we can compute the cosine similarity to the complementary target, and obtain a value to use as a feature of the compositionality of the target. Those features will be used to train a classifier, being the compositionality score of each sample the label to be learnt.

We used RapidMiner[5] (Mierswa et al., 2006) as our Machine Learning framework. The classifiers we have used, that are described below, are the implementations available in RapidMiner.

[3]It would have been possible to consider a common vector space, using all patterns as base vectors. We decided not to do so after realising that a single similarity value for a target and its complementary was not by itself a signal strong enough to predict the compositionality score. A second objective was to assess the relative importance of different syntactic contexts for the task.

[4]We did not attempt any global weighting. We leave this for future work.

[5]`http://rapid-i.com`

2.3 Feature selection

From the 19 original features, inspection of the correlation to the compositionality score label showed that some of them were not to be expected to have much predictive power, while some of them were too sparse in the collection.

We decided to perform feature selection previous to all subsequent learning steps. We used RapidMiner genetic algorithm for feature selection[6]. Among the patterns which features were not selected were those where the $\langle a, n \rangle$ pair appears in prepositional complexes, in noun complexes, as indirect object, as subject or object of the verb to be, and as subject of a possessive. Among those selected were subject and objects of both active and passive constructions, and the object of possessives.

2.4 Runs description

Numeric scores For the numeric evaluation task, we built a regression model by means of a SVM classifier. We used RapidMiner's implementation of mySVMLearner (Rüping, 2000), that is based on the optimization algorithm of SVM-light (Joachims, 1998). We used the default parameters for the classifier. A simple dot product kernel seemed to obtain the best results in 10-fold cross validation over the union of the provided train and validation results. For the three runs, we used identical settings, optimizing different quality measures in each run: absolute error (RUN SCORE-1), Pearson's correlation coefficient (RUN SCORE-2), and Spearman's rho (RUN SCORE-3). The choice of a SVM classifier was motivated by the objective of learning a good parametric classifier model. In initial experiments, SVM showed to perform better than other possible choices, like logistic regression. In hindsight, the relatively small size of the dataset might be a reason for the relatively poor results. Experimenting with other approaches is left for future work.

Coarse scores For the coarse scoring, we decided to build a different set of classifiers, that would learn the nominal 3-valued compositionality label. The classifiers built in our initial experiments turned out

[6]The mutation step switches features on and off, while the crossover step interchanges used features. Selection is done randomly. The algorithm used to evaluate each of the feature subsets was a SVM identical as the one described below.

Run	$avg_\triangle$	r	ρ
RUN-SCORE-1	16.395	0.483	0.487
RUN-SCORE-2	15.874	0.475	0.463
RUN-SCORE-3	16.318	0.494	0.486
baseline	17.857	–	–

Table 1: TRAINING. Numeric score runs results on 10-fold cross-validation for the training set. $avg_\triangle$: average absolute error; r: Pearson's correlation;ρ: Spearman's rho.

Run	$avg_\triangle$	r	ρ
RUN-SCORE-1	17.016	0.237	0.267
RUN-SCORE-2	17.180	0.217	0.219
RUN-SCORE-3	17.289	0.180	0.189
baseline	17.370	–	–

Table 2: TEST. Numeric score runs for the test set. Only for the en-ADJ-NN samples. $avg_\triangle$: average absolute error; r: Pearson's correlation;ρ: Spearman's rho.

to lazily choose the most frequent class ("high") for most of the test samples. In an attempt to overcome this situation and possibly learn non linearly separable classes, we tried neural network classifiers[7]. In hindsight, from seeing the very poor performance of this classifiers on the test set, it is clear that any performance gains were due to over-fitting on the training set.

For RUN COARSE-2, we binned the numeric scores obtained in RUN-SCORE-1, dividing the score space in three equal sized parts; we decided not to assume the same distribution of the three labels for the training and test sets. The results were worse than the numeric scores, due to the fact that the 3 classes are not equally sized.

2.5 Results

Results in the training phase For all our training, we performed 10-fold cross validation. For reference, we report the results as evaluated by averaging over the 10 splits of the union of the provided training and validation set in Table 1. We compared against a dummy baseline: return as constant score the average of the scores in the training and validation sample sets.

Disappointingly, the resulting classifiers seemed to be quite *lazy*, yielding values significatively close to the average of the compositionality label in the training and validation set.

The AutoMNLP and neural network seemed to perform reasonably, and better than other classifiers we tried (e.g., SVM based). We were wary, though, of the risk of having learnt an over-fitted model; unfortunately, the results on the test set confirmed that: for instance, the accuracy of RUN-SCORE-3 for the training set was 0.548, but for the test set it was only 0.327.

Results in the test phase After the task results were distributed, we verified that our numeric score runs, for the subtask en-ADJ-NN performed quite well: fifth among the 17 valid submissions for the subtask, using the average point difference as quality measure. Nevertheless, in terms of ranking correlation scores, our system performs presumably worse, although separate correlation results for the en-ADJ-NN subtask were not available to us at the time of writing this report.

Our naive baseline turns out to be strong in terms of average point score. Of course, the ranking correlation of such a baseline is none; using ranking correlation as quality measure would be more sensible, given that it discards such a baseline.

3 Conclusions

We obtained modest results in the task. Our three numeric runs obtained results very similar to each other. Only taking part in the en-ADJ-NN subtask, we obtained the 5th best of a total of 17 valid systems in average point difference. Nevertheless, in terms ranking correlation scores, our systems seem to perform worse. The modifications we tried to specialize for coarse scoring were unsuccessful, yielding poor results.

A few conclusions we can draw at this moment are: our system could benefit from global frequency weighting schemes that we did not try but that have shown to be successful in the past; the relatively small size of the dataset has not allowed us to learn a better classifier; finally, we believe the ranking correlation quality measures are more sensible than the point difference for this particular task.

[7] For RUN COARSE-1, we used AutoMLP (Breuel and Shafait, 2010), an algorithm that learns a neural network, optimizing both the learning rate and number of hidden nodes of the network. For RUN COARSE-3, we learnt a simple neural network model, by means of a feed-forward neural network trained by a backpropagation algorithm (multi-layer perceptron), with a hidden layer with sigmoid type and size 8.

References

Timothy Baldwin, Colin Bannard, Takaaki Tanaka, and Dominic Widdows. 2003. An empirical model of multiword expression decomposability. In *Proceedings of the ACL 2003 workshop on Multiword expressions: analysis, acquisition and treatment - Volume 18*, MWE '03, pages 89–96, Stroudsburg, PA, USA. Association for Computational Linguistics.

Thomas Breuel and Faisal Shafait. 2010. Automlp: Simple, effective, fully automated learning rate and size adjustment. In *The Learning Workshop*. Online, 4.

Zellig S. Harris. 1954. Distributional structure. *Word*, pages 146–162.

Thorsten Joachims. 1998. Making large-scale svm learning practical. LS8-Report 24, Universität Dortmund, LS VIII-Report.

Graham Katz and Eugenie Giesbrecht. 2006. Automatic identification of non-compositional multi-word expressions using latent semantic analysis. In *Proceedings of the Workshop on Multiword Expressions: Identifying and Exploiting Underlying Properties*, MWE '06, pages 12–19, Stroudsburg, PA, USA. Association for Computational Linguistics.

Ingo Mierswa, Michael Wurst, Ralf Klinkenberg, Martin Scholz, and Timm Euler. 2006. Yale: rapid prototyping for complex data mining tasks. In *KDD'06*, pages 935–940.

Jeff Mitchell and Mirella Lapata. 2010. Composition in distributional models of semantics. *Cognitive Science*, 34(8):1388–1429.

Joakim Nivre and Mario Scholz. 2004. Deterministic dependency parsing of english text. COLING '04.

Sebastian Pado and Mirella Lapata. 2007. Dependency-Based Construction of Semantic Space Models. *Computational Linguistics*, 33(2):161–199, jun.

Anselmo Peñas and Eduard Hovy. 2010. Semantic enrichment of text with background knowledge. pages 15–23, jun.

Stefan Rüping. 2000. mySVM-Manual. `http://www-ai.cs.uni-dortmund.de/SOFTWARE/MYSVM/`.

Peter D. Turney and Patrick Pantel. 2010. From frequency to meaning: Vector space models of semantics. *J. Artif. Intell. Res. (JAIR)*, 37:141–188.

Measuring the compositionality of collocations via word co-occurrence vectors: Shared task system description

Alfredo Maldonado-Guerra and **Martin Emms**
School of Computer Science and Statistics
Trinity College Dublin
Ireland
{maldonaa, mtemms}@scss.tcd.ie

Abstract

A description of a system for measuring the compositionality of collocations within the framework of the shared task of the Distributional Semantics and Compositionality workshop (DISCo 2011) is presented. The system exploits the intuition that a highly compositional collocation would tend to have a considerable semantic overlap with its constituents (headword and modifier) whereas a collocation with low compositionality would share little semantic content with its constituents. This intuition is operationalised via three configurations that exploit cosine similarity measures to detect the semantic overlap between the collocation and its constituents. The system performs competitively in the task.

1 Introduction

Collocations or multiword expressions vary in the degree to which a native speaker is able to understand them based on the interaction of their constituents' individual meanings. The concept of compositionality of a collocation captures this notion. The shared task of the DISCo 2011 workshop (Biemann and Giesbrecht, 2011) consists in comparing systems' compositionality scores against compositionality scores based on human judgements. Systems were evaluated on the match of the compositional scores generated by the system and those based on human judgements – specifically taking the mean of the absolute difference of these scores. Additionally the organisers also classified the human-derived scores into three coarse categories of compositionality: non-compositional (*low*), somewhat compositional (*medium*) and compositional (*high*). Systems were required to produce an additional compositionality labelling into these three coarse categories and were evaluated on the precision of this labelling.

The methods used by our system for measuring compositionality take inspiration from the work of McCarthy et al. (2003), who measured the similarity between a phrasal verb (a main verb and a preposition like *blow up*) and its main verb (*blow*) by comparing the words that are closely semantically related to each, and use this similarity as an indicator of compositionality. Our method for measuring compositionality is considerably different as it instead directly compares the semantic similarity between the headword and the collocation and between the modifier and the collocation by computing a cosine similarity score between word co-occurrence vectors that represent the headword, the modifier and the collocation (see 3.2). Our system can be regarded as fully unsupervised as it does not employ any parsers in its processing or any external data other than the corpus and the collocation lists provided by the organisers.

The rest of the paper is organised as follows: Section 2 describes the corpora and the collocation list provided by the task organisers. Section 3 introduces some definitions and describes the three configurations in detail. Section 4 presents the results and concludes.

2 Data

Shared task participants were provided with a list of collocations of three grammatical forms: adjective-

Proceedings of the Workshop on Distributional Semantics and Compositionality (DiSCo'2011), pages 48–53,
Portland, Oregon, 24 June 2011.

noun collocations (**A-N**), subject-verb collocations (**S-V**) and verb-object collocations (**V-O**). Our system assumes that each collocation consists of a headword and a modifier and it interprets these constituents in each grammatical form as follows: **A-N**: adjective - modifier, noun - headword; **S-V**: subject - modifier, verb - headword; **V-O**: verb - headword, object - modifier.

As a corpus, our system uses a random sample of 500,000 documents from the plain-text, non-parsed version of the English ukWaC corpus (Baroni et al., 2009).

3 System description

Our system can be employed in three different configurations. All three rely in representing words and collocations as word co-occurrence vectors and measure semantic similarity using the cosine measure.

3.1 Preliminary definitions

These definitions are largely based on the construction of first-order context vectors, word co-occurrence vectors and second-order context vectors via global selection as described in Schütze (1998) and in Purandare and Pedersen (2004) by considering context windows of 20 words centred at a target word.

The **first-order context vector** is a vector representing a *token* of a word, or equivalently a *position* p in a document. Dimensions of the vector are word types w, and the value on dimension w *is a count of the frequency with which w occurs in a specified window around p in a given document doc.*

$$\mathbf{C^1}(p)(w) = \sum_{\substack{p' \neq p \\ p-10 \leq p' \\ p' \leq p+10}} (1 \text{ if } w = \text{doc}(p'), \text{ else } 0) \quad (1)$$

In this work the dimensions are the 2,000 non-function words that are most frequent in the corpus[1]. The **word co-occurrence vector** (or simply **word vector**) is a vector recording the co-occurrence behaviour of a particular word *type* w in a corpus. As such it can be defined by summation over first-order context vectors:

$$\mathbf{W}(w) = \sum_p (1 \text{ if } w = \text{doc}(p), \text{ else } 0) \cdot \mathbf{C^1}(p) \quad (2)$$

And the **second-order context vector** is a further vector representing an instance of a word. For a particular location p, it is defined to be *sum of the word vectors of words in a given window around p*

$$\mathbf{C^2}(p) = \sum_{\substack{p' \neq p \\ p-10 \leq p' \\ p' \leq p+10}} \mathbf{W}(\text{doc}(p)) \quad (3)$$

Although the above are defined for types and tokens of *words*, they can be generalised to *multiword* expressions in various ways. In this work, for any multiword expression *type* $x\ y$, its *tokens* are taken to be occurrences of the sequence $x\gamma y$, where γ can be any sequence of intervening words of length l, $0 \leq l \leq 3$. By taking the position of x as the position of the multiword token, and taking the first position after the token as position $p+1$, the definitions of $\mathbf{C^1}$, $\mathbf{W}$ and $\mathbf{C^2}$ can be carried over to multiword expressions.

All the configurations described below use the cosine measure between vectors, defined in the standard way

$$\cos(\mathbf{v}, \mathbf{w}) = \frac{\sum_{i=1}^{N} v_i w_i}{\sqrt{\sum_{i=1}^{N} v_i^2 \sum_{i=1}^{N} w_i^2}} \quad (4)$$

3.2 System configurations

For each collocation in the test set, the **first configuration** of our system starts off by building word vectors for the collocation, its headword and its modifier.

The first configuration of the system outputs the average of two cosine similarity measures as the compositionality score for the collocation:

$$c_1 = \frac{1}{2} \begin{bmatrix} \cos(\mathbf{W}(xy), \mathbf{W}(x)) \\ + \cos(\mathbf{W}(xy), \mathbf{W}(y)) \end{bmatrix} \quad (5)$$

where $\mathbf{W}(xy)$ is the word vector representing the collocation whose constituents are x and y, and $\mathbf{W}(x)$ and $\mathbf{W}(y)$ are the word vectors representing each constituent x and y, respectively.

[1]We employ a modified version of the stop word list supplied with Ted Pedersen's Text-NSP package (http://www.d.umn.edu/~tpederse/nsp.html)

The **second configuration** of our system considers the occurrences of the headword when accompanied by the modifier forming the collocation separately from occurrences of the headword appearing on its own and compares them. If y is the headword of a collocation and $\text{coll}(p)$ is a Boolean function that determines whether the word at position p forms a collocation with x, let

$$\mathbf{W}^{x}(y) = \sum_{p} (1 \text{ if } \substack{\text{doc}(p) = y \\ \text{coll}(p,x)}, \text{ else } 0) \cdot \mathbf{C}^{1}(p) \quad (6)$$

be the word vector computed from all the occurrences of the headword y that form a collocation with x and conversely, let

$$\mathbf{W}^{\bar{x}}(y) = \sum_{p} (1 \text{ if } \substack{\text{doc}(p) = y \\ \neg\text{coll}(p,x)}, \text{ else } 0) \cdot \mathbf{C}^{1}(p) \quad (7)$$

be the word vector representing the occurrences of y not engaging in a collocation with x. In this configuration, the compositionality score is then computed by

$$c_2 = \cos\left(\mathbf{W}^{x}(y), \mathbf{W}^{\bar{x}}(y)\right) \quad (8)$$

The intuition behind this configuration is that if the headword tends to co-occur with more or less the same words in both cases (producing a high cosine score), then the meaning of the headword is similar regardless of whether the collocation's modifier is present or not, implying a high degree of compositionality. If on the other hand, the headword co-occurs with somewhat differing words in the two cases (a low cosine score), then we assume that the presence of the collocation's modifier is markedly changing the meaning of the headword, implying a low degree of compositionality.

In its **third configuration**, our system employs clustering techniques in order to exploit semantic differences that may naturally emerge from each context in which the collocation and its constituents are used. Different senses of a collocation might have different compositionality measures as can be seen in these two example sentences employing the collocation *great deal*:

1. Two cans of soup for the price of one is such a *great deal*!

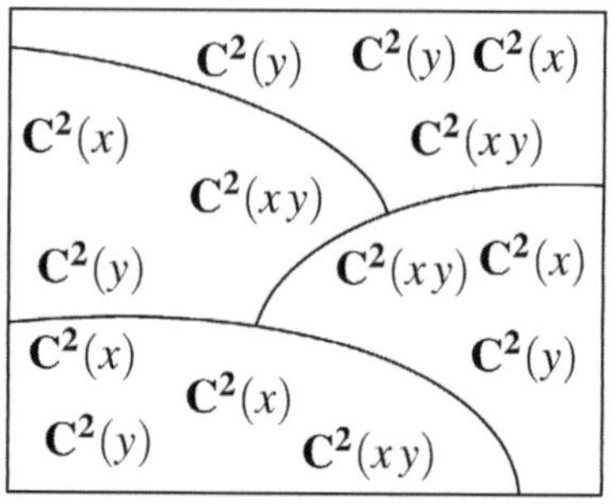

Figure 1: *Example of a clustered second-order context vector space.*

2. The tsunami caused a *great deal* of damage to the country's infrastructure.

In Word Sense Induction, clustering is used to group occurrences of a target word according to its sense or usage in context (see e.g. Pedersen (2010)) as it is expected that each cluster will represent a different sense or usage of the target word. However, since the contexts that human annotators referred to when judging the compositionality of the collocations was not provided, our system employs a workaround that uses a weighted average when measuring compositionality. This workaround is explained in what follows.

In this configuration, the system first builds word vectors for the 20,000 most frequent words in the corpus (equation 2), and then uses these to compute the second-order context vectors for each occurrence of the collocation and its constituents in the corpus (equation 3). After context vectors for all occurrences have been computed, they are clustered using CLUTO's repeated bisections algorithm[2]. The vectors are clustered across a small number K of clusters (we employed $K = 4$). We expect that each cluster will represent a different contextual usage of the collocation, its headword and its modifier. Figure 1 depicts how a context vector space could be partitioned with $K = 4$.

The system then for each cluster k builds the word vectors (equation 2) $\mathbf{W}_k(x\,y)$, $\mathbf{W}_k(x)$, and $\mathbf{W}_k(y)$ for the collocation, its headword and its modifier, from the contexts grouped within the cluster k. The compositionality measure for the third configuration is then basically a weighted average over the clusters

[2]http://glaros.dtc.umn.edu/gkhome/views/cluto/

of the c_1 score using each cluster, that is:

$$c_3 = \sum_{k=1}^{K} \frac{\|k\|}{N} \frac{1}{2} \left[\begin{array}{l} \cos(\mathbf{W}_k(x\,y), \mathbf{W}_k(x)) \\ +\cos(\mathbf{W}_k(x\,y), \mathbf{W}_k(y)) \end{array} \right] \quad (9)$$

where $\|k\|$ is the number of contexts in cluster k and N is the total number of contexts across all clusters.

For all three configurations, the value reported as the numeric compositionality score was the corresponding value obtained from equations (5), (8) or (9), multiplied by 100. Each configuration's numeric scores c_i were binned into the three coarse compositionality classes by comparing them with the configuration's maximum value through equation (10).

$$\text{coarse}(c_i) = \begin{cases} high & \text{if } \frac{2}{3}max \leq c_i \\ medium & \text{if } \frac{1}{3}max < c_i < \frac{2}{3}max \\ low & \text{if } c_i \leq \frac{1}{3}max \end{cases} \quad (10)$$

4 Results and conclusion

Table 1 shows the evaluation results for the three system configurations and two baselines. The left-hand side of the table shows the average difference between the gold-standard numeric score and each configuration's numeric score. The right-hand side reports the precision on binning the numeric scores into the coarse classes. Evaluation scores are reported on all collocations and on the collocation subtypes separately. Row **R** is the baseline suggested by the workshop organisers, assigning random numeric scores, in turn binned into the coarse categories. Row **A** shows the performance of a constant output baseline, assigning all collocations the *mean* gold-standard numeric score from the training set: 66.45, and then applying the binning strategy of equation (10) to this – which always assigns the coarse category *high*.

The first thing to note from this table is that configurations 1 and 2 generally outperform configuration 3, both on the mean difference and coarse scores. Configuration 1 slightly outperforms configuration 2 on the mean numeric difference scores, whilst configuration 2 is very close to and slightly better than configuration 1 on the coarse precision scores. The exception is that configuration 3 was the best performer on the coarse precision scoring for the **S-V** subtype.

C	Average differences (numeric)				Precision (coarse)			
	ALL	A-N	S-V	V-O	ALL	A-N	S-V	V-O
1	**17.95**	**18.56**	20.80	**15.58**	53.4	**63.5**	19.2	62.5
2	18.35	19.62	**20.20**	15.73	**54.2**	**63.5**	19.2	**65.0**
3	25.59	24.16	32.04	23.73	44.9	40.4	**42.3**	52.5
R	32.82	34.57	29.83	32.34	29.7	28.8	30.0	30.8
A	16.86	17.73	15.54	16.52	58.5	65.4	34.6	65.0

Table 1: *Evaluation results of the three system configurations and two baselines on the test dataset. Best system scores on each grammatical subtype highlighted in bold.*

The R baseline is outperformed by configurations 1, 2 and 3; roughly speaking where 1 and 2 outperform R by d, configuration 3 outperforms R by around $d/2$. The A baseline generally outperforms all our system configurations. It seems to be also a quite competitive baseline for other systems participating in the shared task.

The other trend apparent from the table is that performance on the **V-O** and **A-N** subtypes tends to exceed that on the the **S-V** subtype.

An examination of the gold standard test files shows that the distribution over the *low*/*medium*/*high* categories is similar for both **V-O** and **A-N**, in both cases close to 0.08/0.27/0.65, with *high* covering nearly two-thirds of cases, whilst for **S-V** the distribution is quite different: 0.0/0.654/0.346, with *medium* covering nearly two-thirds of cases. This is reflected in the A baseline precision scores, as for each subtype these will necessarily be the proportion of gold-standard *high* cases. This explains for example why the A baseline is much poorer on the **S-V** cases (34.6) than on the other cases (65.0, 65.4).

Looking further into the differences between the three subtypes, Figure 2 shows the gold standard numeric score distribution across the three collocation subtypes (**Test GS**), and the corresponding distributions for scores from the system's first configuration (**Conf 1**). This shows in more detail the nature of the poorer performance on **S-V**, with the gold standard having a peak around 50-60, and the system having a peak around 70-80. For the other subtypes

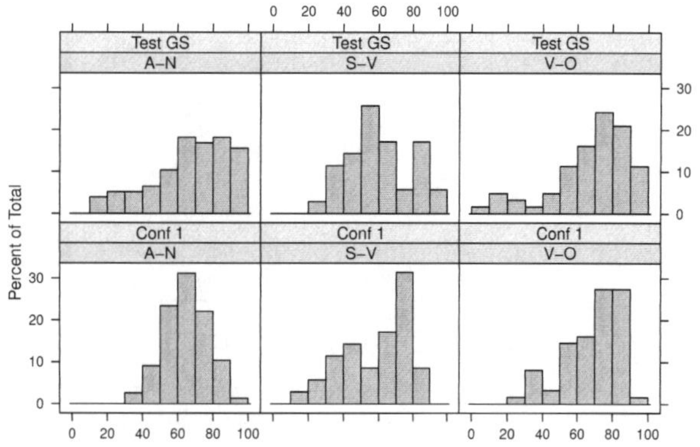

Figure 2: *The distribution of the gold standard numeric score vs. the distribution of the system's first configuration numeric scores.*

	A-N	S-V	V-O
Instances	177254	11092	121317
Avg intervening	0.0684	0.3867	0.4612

Table 2: *Some corpus statistics: the number of matched collocations per subtype (**Instances**) and the average number of intervening words per subtype (**Avg intervening**).*

the contrast in the distributions seems broadly consistent with the mean numeric difference scores of Table 1.

One can speculate on the reasons for the system's poorer performance on the **S-V** subtype. The system treats intervening words in a collocation in a particular way, namely by ignoring them. This is one option, and another would be to include them as features counted in the vectors. Table 2 shows the average intervening words in the occurrences of the collocations. **S-V** and **V-O** are alike in this respect, both being much more likely to present intervening words than collocations of the **A-N** subtype. So the explanation of the poorer performance on **S-V** cannot lie there. Also because the average number of intervening words is low, we believe it is unlikely that including them as features will impact performance significantly.

Table 2 also gives the number of matched collocations per subtype. The number for the **S-V** collocations is an order of magnitude smaller than for the other subtypes. Although the collocations supplied by the organisers are in their base form, the system attempts to match them 'as is' in the unlemmatised version of the corpus. Whilst for **A-N** and **V-O** the base-form sequences relatively frequently do double service as inflected forms, this is far less frequently the case for the **S-V** sequences (e.g. *user see* (**S-V**) is far less common than *make money* (**V-O**)). This much smaller number of occurrences for **S-V** cases, or the fact that they are drawn from syntactically special contexts, may be a factor in the relatively poorer performance. This perhaps is also a factor in the earlier noted fact that although configuration 3 was generally outperformed, on the **S-V** subtype the reverse occurs.

The unlemmatised version of the corpus was used because initial experimentation with the validation set produced slightly better results when employing raw words as features rather than lemmas. A possibility for future work would be to to refer to lemmas for matching collocations in the corpus, but to continue to use unlemmatised words as features.

Other areas for future investigation involve the effects of weighting schemes (such as IDF) and the use of similarity measures other than cosine, as well as alternatives in configurations 2 and 3. For example, configuration 2 could involve the modifier in the computation of the compositionality score, and configuration 3 could create separate clustering spaces for collocation, headword and modifier and compute similarity scores based on vectors representing these clusters.

In sum, the simplest configuration of a totally unsupervised system yielded surprisingly good results at measuring compositionality of collocations in raw corpora, and whereas there is scope for further development and refinement, the system as it is constitutes a robust baseline to compare against more elaborate systems.

5 Acknowledgements

We would like to thank our anonymous reviewers for their insightful comments and ideas. This research is supported by the Science Foundation Ireland (Grant 07/CE/I1142) as part of the Centre for Next Generation Localisation (www.cngl.ie) at Trinity College Dublin.

References

Marco Baroni, Silvia Bernardini, Adriano Ferraresi, and Eros Zanchetta. 2009. The WaCky wide web: a collection of very large linguistically processed web-crawled corpora. *Language Resources and Evaluation*, 43(3):209–226, February.

Chris Biemann and Eugenie Giesbrecht. 2011. Distributional Semantics and Compositionality 2011: Shared Task Description and Results. In *Proceedings of the Distributional Semantics and Compositionality workshop (DISCo 2011) in conjunction with ACL 2011*, Portland, Oregon.

Diana McCarthy, Bill Keller, and John Carroll. 2003. Detecting a continuum of compositionality in phrasal verbs. In *Proceedings of the ACL 2003 workshop on Multiword expressions: analysis, acquisition and treatment-Volume 18*, pages 73–80, Sapporo. Association for Computational Linguistics.

Ted Pedersen. 2010. Duluth-WSI: SenseClusters applied to the sense induction task of SemEval-2. In *Proceedings of the 5th International Workshop on Semantic Evaluation*, number July, pages 363–366, Uppsala, Sweden. Association for Computational Linguistics.

Amruta Purandare and Ted Pedersen. 2004. Word sense discrimination by clustering contexts in vector and similarity spaces. *Proceedings of the Conference on Computational Natural Language Learning*, pages 41–48.

Hinrich Schütze. 1998. Automatic word sense discrimination. *Computational Linguistics*, 24(1):97–123.

Exemplar-based Word-Space Model for Compositionality Detection: Shared task system description

Siva Reddy
University of York, UK
siva@cs.york.ac.uk

Diana McCarthy
Lexical Computing Ltd, UK
diana@dianamccarthy.co.uk

Suresh Manandhar
University of York, UK
suresh@cs.york.ac.uk

Spandana Gella
University of York, UK
spandana@cs.york.ac.uk

Abstract

In this paper, we highlight the problems of polysemy in word space models of compositionality detection. Most models represent each word as a single prototype-based vector without addressing polysemy. We propose an exemplar-based model which is designed to handle polysemy. This model is tested for compositionality detection and it is found to outperform existing prototype-based models. We have participated in the shared task (Biemann and Giesbrecht, 2011) and our best performing exemplar-model is ranked first in two types of evaluations and second in two other evaluations.

1 Introduction

In the field of computational semantics, to represent the meaning of a compound word, two mechanisms are commonly used. One is based on *the distributional hypothesis* (Harris, 1954) and the other is on *the principle of semantic compositionality* (Partee, 1995, p. 313).

The distributional hypothesis (DH) states that words that occur in similar contexts tend to have similar meanings. Using this hypothesis, distributional models like the Word-space model (WSM, Sahlgren, 2006) represent a target word's meaning as a *context vector* (location in space). The similarity between two meanings is the *closeness* (proximity) between the vectors. The context vector of a target word is built from its distributional behaviour observed in a corpus. Similarly, the context vector of a compound word can be built by treating the compound as a single word. We refer to such a vector as a DH-based vector.

The other mechanism is based on the principle of semantic compositionality (PSC) which states that the meaning of a compound word is a function of, and only of, the meaning of its parts and the way in which the parts are combined. If the meaning of a part is represented in a WSM using the distributional hypothesis, then the principle can be applied to compose the distributional behaviour of a compound word from its parts without actually using the corpus instances of the compound. We refer to this as a PSC-based vector. So a PSC-based is composed of component DH-based vectors.

Both of these two mechanisms are capable of determining the meaning vector of a compound word. For a given compound, if a DH-based vector and a PSC-based vector of the compound are projected into an identical space, one would expect the vectors to occupy the same location i.e. both the vectors should be nearly the same. However the principle of semantic compositionality does not hold for non-compositional compounds, which is actually what the existing WSMs of compositionality detection exploit (Giesbrecht, 2009; Katz and Giesbrecht, 2006; Schone and Jurafsky, 2001). The DH-based and PSC-based vectors are expected to have high similarity when a compound is compositional and low similarity for non-compositional compounds.

Most methods in WSM (Turney and Pantel, 2010) represent a word as a single context vector built from merging all its corpus instances. Such a representation is called the *prototype-based* modelling (Murphy, 2002). These prototype-based vectors do not

Proceedings of the Workshop on Distributional Semantics and Compositionality (DiSCo'2011), pages 54–60,
Portland, Oregon, 24 June 2011. ©2011 Association for Computational Linguistics

distinguish the instances according to the senses of a target word. Since most compounds are less ambiguous than single words, there is less need for distinguishing instances in a DH-based prototype vector of a compound and we do not address that here but leave ambiguity of compounds for future work. However the constituent words of the compound are more ambiguous. When DH-based vectors of the constituent words are used for composing the PSC-based vector of the compound, the resulting vector may contain instances, and therefore contexts, that are not relevant for the given compound. These noisy contexts effect the similarity between the PSC-based vector and the DH-based vector of the compound. Basing compositionality judgements on a such a noisy similarity value is no longer reliable.

In this paper, we address this problem of polysemy of constituent words of a compound using an exemplar-based modelling (Smith and Medin, 1981). In exemplar-based modelling of WSM (Erk and Padó, 2010), each word is represented by all its corpus instances (*exemplars*) without merging them into a single vector. Depending upon the purpose, only relevant exemplars of the target word are activated and then these are merged to form a refined prototype-vector which is less-noisy compared to the original prototype-vector. Exemplar-based models are more powerful than prototype-based ones because they retain specific instance information.

We have evaluated our models on the validation data released in the shared task (Biemann and Giesbrecht, 2011). Based on the validation results, we have chosen three systems for public evaluation and participated in the shared task (Biemann and Giesbrecht, 2011).

2 Word Space Model

In this section, construction of WSM for all our experiments is described. We use Sketch Engine[1] (Kilgarriff et al., 2004) to retrieve all the exemplars for a target word or a pattern using corpus query language. Let $w_1\ w_2$ be a compound word with constituent words w_1 and w_2. E_w denotes the set of exemplars of w. V_w is the prototype vector of the word w, which is built by merging all the exemplars in E_w

For the purposes of producing a PSC-based vector for a compound, a vector of a constituent word is built using only the exemplars which *do not* contain the compound. Note that the vectors are sensitive to a compound's word-order since the exemplars of $w_1\ w_2$ are not the same as $w_2\ w_1$.

We use other WSM settings following Mitchell and Lapata (2008). The dimensions of the WSM are the top 2000 content words in the given corpus (along with their coarse-grained part-of-speech information). Cosine similarity (sim) is used to measure the similarity between two vectors. Values at the specific positions in the vector representing context words are set to the ratio of the probability of the context word given the target word to the overall probability of the context word. The context window of a target word's exemplar is the whole sentence of the target word excluding the target word. Our language of interest is English. We use the ukWaC corpus (Ferraresi et al., 2008) for producing out WSMs.

3 Related Work

As described in Section 1, most WSM models for compositionality detection measure the similarity between the true distributional vector $V_{w_1w_2}$ of the compound and the composed vector $V_{w_1 \oplus w_2}$, where $\oplus$ denotes a compositionality function. If the similarity is high, the compound is treated as compositional or else non-compositional.

Giesbrecht (2009); Katz and Giesbrecht (2006); Schone and Jurafsky (2001) obtained the compositionality vector of $w_1\ w_2$ using vector addition $V_{w_1 \oplus w_2} = aV_{w_1} + bV_{w_2}$. In this approach, if $sim(V_{w_1 \oplus w_2}, V_{w_1w_2}) > \gamma$, the compound is classified as compositional, where γ is a threshold for deciding compositionality. Global values of a and b were chosen by optimizing the performance on the development set. It was found that no single threshold value γ held for all compounds. Changing the threshold alters performance arbitrarily. This might be due to the polysemous nature of the constituent words which makes the composed vector $V_{w_1 \oplus w_2}$ filled with noisy contexts and thus making the judgement unpredictable.

In the above model, if a=0 and b=1, the resulting model is similar to that of Baldwin et al. (2003). They also observe similar behaviour of the thresh-

[1]Sketch Engine `http://www.sketchengine.co.uk`

old γ. We try to address this problem by addressing the polysemy in WSMs using exemplar-based modelling.

The above models use a simple addition based compositionality function. Mitchell and Lapata (2008) observed that a simple multiplication function modelled compositionality better than addition. Contrary to that, Guevara (2011) observed additive models worked well for building compositional vectors. In our work, we try using evidence from both compositionality functions, simple addition and simple multiplication.

Bannard et al. (2003); McCarthy et al. (2003) observed that methods based on distributional similarities between a phrase and its constituent words help when determining the compositionality behaviour of phrases. We therefore also use evidence from the similarities between each constituent word and the compound.

4 Our Approach: Exemplar-based Model

Our approach works as follows. Firstly, given a compound $w_1\ w_2$, we build its DH-based prototype vector $V_{w_1w_2}$ from all its exemplars $E_{w_1w_2}$. Secondly, we remove irrelevant exemplars in E_{w_1} and E_{w_2} of constituent words and build the refined prototype vectors $V_{w_1^r}$ and $V_{w_2^r}$ of the constituent words w_1 and w_2 respectively. These refined vectors are used to compose the PSC-based vectors [2] of the compound. Related work to ours is (Reisinger and Mooney, 2010) where exemplars of a word are first clustered and then prototype vectors are built. This work does not relate to compositionality but to measuring semantic similarity of single words. As such, their clusters are not influenced by other words whereas in our approach for detecting compositionality, the other constituent word plays a major role.

We use the compositionality functions, simple addition and simple multiplication to build $V_{w_1^r+w_2^r}$ and $V_{w_1^r\times w_2^r}$ respectively. Based on the similarities $sim(V_{w_1w_2}, V_{w_1^r})$, $sim(V_{w_1w_2}, V_{w_2^r})$, $sim(V_{w_1w_2}, V_{w_1^r+w_2^r})$ and $sim(V_{w_1w_2}, V_{w_1^r\times w_2^r})$, we decide if the compound is compositional or non-compositional. These steps are described in a little more detail below.

[2]Note that we use two PSC-based vectors for representing a compound.

4.1 Building Refined Prototype Vectors

We aim to remove irrelevant exemplars of one constituent word with the help of the other constituent word's distributional behaviour. For example, let us take the compound *traffic light*. *Light* occurs in many contexts such as quantum theory, optics, lamps and spiritual theory. In ukWaC, $light$ has 316,126 instances. Not all these exemplars are relevant to compose the PSC-based vector of *traffic light*. These irrelevant exemplars increases the semantic differences between *traffic light* and *light* and thus increase the differences between $V_{\text{traffic}\oplus\text{light}}$ and $V_{\text{traffic light}}$. $sim(V_{\text{light}}, V_{\text{traffic light}})$ is found to be 0.27.

Our intuition and motivation for exemplar removal is that it is beneficiary to choose only the exemplars of *light* which share similar contexts of *traffic* since *traffic light* should have contexts similar to both *traffic* and *light* if it is compositional. We rank each exemplar of *light* based on common co-occurrences of *traffic* and also words which are distributionally similar to *traffic*. Co-occurrences of *traffic* are the context words which frequently occur with *traffic*, e.g. car, road etc. Using these, the exemplar from a sentence such as "*Cameras capture **cars** running red **lights** ...*" will be ranked higher than one which does not have contexts related to *traffic*. The distributionally similar words to *traffic* are the words (like synonyms, antonyms) which are similar to *traffic* in that they occur in similar contexts, e.g. transport, flow etc. Using these distributionally similar words helps reduce the impact of data sparseness and helps prioritise contexts of *traffic* which are semantically related. We use Sketch Engine to compute the scores of a word observed in a given corpus. Sketch Engine scores the co-occurrences (collocations) using logDice motivated by (Curran, 2003) and distributionally related words using (Rychlý and Kilgarriff, 2007; Lexical Computing Ltd., 2007). For a given word, both of these scores are normalised in the range (0,1)

All the exemplars of *light* are ranked based on the co-occurrences of these collocations and distributionally related words of *traffic* using

$$s^{\text{traffic}}_{E\,\in\,E_{\text{light}}} = \sum_{c\,\in\,E} x^E_c \times y^{\text{traffic}}_c \quad (1)$$

where $s^{\text{traffic}}_{E\,\in\,E_{\text{light}}}$ stands for the relevance score of the exemplar E w.r.t. *traffic*, c for context word in the exemplar E, x_c^E is the coordinate value (contextual score) of the context word c in the exemplar E and y_c^{traffic} is the score of the context word c w.r.t. *traffic*.

A refined prototype vector of *light* is then built by merging the top *n* exemplars of *light*

$$V_{\text{light}^r} = \sum_{e_i \in E_{\text{light}}^{\text{traffic}}; i=0}^{n} e_i \quad (2)$$

where $E_{\text{light}}^{\text{traffic}}$ are the set of exemplars of *light* ranked using co-occurrence information from the other constituent word *traffic*. n is chosen such that $sim(V_{\text{light}^r}, V_{\text{traffic light}})$ is maximised. This similarity is observed to be greatest using just 2286 (less than 1%) of the total exemplars of *light*. After exemplar removal, $sim(V_{\text{light}^r}, V_{\text{traffic light}})$ increased to 0.47 from the initial value of 0.27. Though n is chosen by maximising similarity, which is not desirable for non-compositional compounds, the lack of similarity will give the strongest possible indication that a compound is not compositional.

4.2 Building Compositional Vectors

We use the compositionality functions, simple addition and simple multiplication to build compositional vectors $V_{w_1^r+w_2^r}$ and $V_{w_1^r \times w_2^r}$. These are as described in (Mitchell and Lapata, 2008). In model addition, $V_{w_1 \oplus w_2} = aV_{w_1} + bV_{w_2}$, all the previous approaches use static values of a and b. Instead, we use dynamic weights computed from the participating vectors using $a = \frac{sim(V_{w_1w_2}, V_{w_1})}{sim(V_{w_1w_2}, V_{w_1}) + sim(V_{w_1w_2}, V_{w_2})}$ and $b = 1 - a$. These weights differ from compound to compound.

4.3 Compositionality Judgement

To judge if a compound is compositional or non-compositional, previous approaches (see Section 3) base their judgement on a single similarity value. As discussed, we base our judgement based on the collective evidences from all the similarity values using a linear equation of the form

$$\begin{aligned}\alpha(V_{w_1^r}, V_{w_2^r}) &= a_0 + a_1.sim(V_{w_1w_2}, V_{w_1^r}) \\ &+ a_2.sim(V_{w_1w_2}, V_{w_2^r}) \\ &+ a_3.sim(V_{w_1w_2}, V_{w_1^r+w_2^r}) \\ &+ a_4.sim(V_{w_1w_2}, V_{w_1^r \times w_2^r})\end{aligned} \quad (3)$$

Model	APD	Acc.
Exm-Best	13.09	88.0
Pro-Addn	15.42	76.0
Pro-Mult	17.52	80.0
Pro-Best	15.12	80.0

Table 1: Average Point Difference (APD) and Average Accuracy (Acc.) of Compositionality Judgements

where the value of α denotes the compositionality score. The range of α is in between 0-100. If $\alpha \leq 34$, the compound is treated as non-compositional, $34 < \alpha < 67$ as medium compositional and $\alpha \geq 67$ as highly compositional. The parameters a_i's are estimated using ordinary least square regression by training over the training data released in the shared task (Biemann and Giesbrecht, 2011). For the three categories – adjective-noun, verb-object and subject-verb – the parameters are estimated separately.

Note that if $a_1 = a_2 = a_4 = 0$, the model bases its judgement only on addition. Similarly if $a_1 = a_2 = a_3 = 0$, the model bases its judgement only on multiplication.

We also experimented with combinations such as $\alpha(V_{w_1^r}, V_{w_2})$ and $\alpha(V_{w_1}, V_{w_2^r})$ i.e. using refined vector for one of the constituent word and the unrefined prototype vector for the other constituent word.

4.4 Selecting the best model

To participate in the shared task, we have selected the best performing model by evaluating the models on the validation data released in the shared task (Biemann and Giesbrecht, 2011). Table 1 displays the results on the validation data. The average point difference is calculated by taking the average of the difference in a model's score α and the gold score annotated by humans, over all compounds. Table 1 also displays the overall accuracy of coarse grained labels – low, medium and high.

Best performance for verb(v)-object(o) compounds is found for the combination $\alpha(V_{v^r}, V_{o^r})$ of Equation 3. For subject(s)-verb(v) compounds, it is for $\alpha(V_{s^r}, V_{v^r})$ and $a_3 = a_4 = 0$. For adjective(j)-noun(n) compounds, it is $\alpha(V_{j^r}, V_n)$. We are not certain of the reason for this difference, perhaps there may be less ambiguity of words within specific grammatical relationships or it may be simply due to

	TotPrd	Spearman ρ	Kendalls τ
Rand-Base	174	0.02	0.02
Exm-Best	169	**0.35**	**0.24**
Pro-Best	169	0.33	0.23
Exm	169	0.26	0.18
SharedTaskNextBest	174	0.33	0.23

Table 2: Correlation Scores

the actual compounds in those categories. We leave analysis of this for future work. We combined the outputs of these category-specific models to build the best model *Exm-Best*.

For comparison, results of standard models prototype addition *(Pro-Addn)* and prototype-multiplication *(Pro-Mult)* are also displayed in Table 1. *Pro-Addn* can be represented as $\alpha(V_{w_1}, V_{w_2})$ with $a_1 = a_2 = a_4 = 0$. *Pro-Mult* can be represented as $\alpha(V_{w_1}, V_{w_2})$ with $a_1 = a_2 = a_3 = 0$. *Pro-Best* is the best performing model in prototype-based modelling. It is found to be $\alpha(V_{w_1}, V_{w_2})$. (Note: Depending upon the compound type, some of the a_i's in *Pro-Best* may be 0).

Overall, exemplar-based modelling excelled in both the evaluations, average point difference and coarse-grained label accuracies. The systems *Exm-Best*, *Pro-Best* and *Exm* $\alpha(V_{w_1^r}, V_{w_2^r})$ were submitted for the public evaluation in the shared task. All the model parameters were estimated by regression on the task's training data separately for the 3 compound types as described in Section 4.3. We perform the regression separately for these classes to maximise performance. In the future, we will investigate whether these settings gave us better results on the test data compared to setting the values the same regardless of the category of compound.

5 Shared Task Results

Table 2 displays Spearman ρ and Kendalls τ correlation scores of all the models. TotPrd stands for the total number of predictions. Rand-Base is the baseline system which randomly assigns a compositionality score for a compound. Our model Exm-Best was the best performing system compared to all other systems in this evaluation criteria. Shared-TaskNextBest is the next best performing system apart from our models. Due to lemmatization errors in the test data, our models could only predict judgements for 169 out of 174 compounds.

	All	ADJ-NN	V-SUBJ	V-OBJ
Rand-Base	32.82	34.57	29.83	32.34
Zero-Base	23.42	24.67	17.03	25.47
Exm-Best	**16.51**	15.19	15.72	18.6
Pro-Best	16.79	14.62	18.89	18.31
Exm	17.28	15.82	18.18	18.6
SharedTaskBest	**16.19**	14.93	21.64	14.66

Table 3: Average Point Difference Scores

	All	ADJ-NN	V-SUBJ	V-OBJ
Rand-Base	0.297	0.288	0.308	0.30
Zero-Base	0.356	0.288	0.654	0.25
Most-Freq-Base	0.593	0.673	0.346	0.65
Exm-Best	**0.576**	0.692	0.5	0.475
Pro-Best	0.567	0.731	0.346	0.5
Exm	0.542	0.692	0.346	0.475
SharedTaskBest	**0.585**	0.654	0.385	0.625

Table 4: Coarse Grained Accuracy

Table 3 displays average point difference scores. Zero-Base is a baseline system which assigns a score of 50 to all compounds. SharedTaskBest is the overall best performing system. Exm-Best was ranked second best among all the systems. For ADJ-NN and V-SUBJ compounds, the best performing systems in the shared task are Pro-Best and Exm-Best respectively. Our models did less well on V-OBJ compounds and we will explore the reasons for this in future work.

Table 4 displays coarse grained scores. As above, similar behaviour is observed for coarse grained accuracies. Most-Freq-Base is the baseline system which assigns the most frequent coarse-grained label for a compound based on its type (ADJ-NN, V-SUBJ, V-OBJ) as observed in training data. Most-Freq-Base outperforms all other systems.

6 Conclusions

In this paper, we examined the effect of polysemy in word space models for compositionality detection. We showed exemplar-based WSM is effective in dealing with polysemy. Also, we use multiple evidences for compositionality detection rather than basing our judgement on a single evidence. Overall, performance of the Exemplar-based models of compositionality detection is found to be superior to prototype-based models.

References

Baldwin, T., Bannard, C., Tanaka, T., and Widdows, D. (2003). An empirical model of multiword expression decomposability. In *Proceedings of the ACL 2003 workshop on Multiword expressions: analysis, acquisition and treatment - Volume 18*, MWE '03, pages 89–96, Stroudsburg, PA, USA. Association for Computational Linguistics.

Bannard, C., Baldwin, T., and Lascarides, A. (2003). A statistical approach to the semantics of verb-particles. In *Proceedings of the ACL 2003 workshop on Multiword expressions: analysis, acquisition and treatment - Volume 18*, MWE '03, pages 65–72, Stroudsburg, PA, USA. Association for Computational Linguistics.

Biemann, C. and Giesbrecht, E. (2011). Distributional semantics and compositionality 2011: Shared task description and results. In *Proceedings of DISCo-2011 in conjunction with ACL 2011*.

Curran, J. R. (2003). From distributional to semantic similarity. Technical report, PhD Thesis, University of Edinburgh.

Erk, K. and Padó, S. (2010). Exemplar-based models for word meaning in context. In *Proceedings of the ACL 2010 Conference Short Papers*, ACLShort '10, pages 92–97, Stroudsburg, PA, USA. Association for Computational Linguistics.

Ferraresi, A., Zanchetta, E., Baroni, M., and Bernardini, S. (2008). Introducing and evaluating ukwac, a very large web-derived corpus of english. In *Proceedings of the WAC4 Workshop at LREC 2008*, Marrakesh, Morocco.

Giesbrecht, E. (2009). In search of semantic compositionality in vector spaces. In *Proceedings of the 17th International Conference on Conceptual Structures: Conceptual Structures: Leveraging Semantic Technologies*, ICCS '09, pages 173–184, Berlin, Heidelberg. Springer-Verlag.

Guevara, E. R. (2011). Computing semantic compositionality in distributional semantics. In *Proceedings of the Ninth International Conference on Computational Semantics*, IWCS '2011.

Harris, Z. S. (1954). Distributional structure. *Word*, 10:146–162.

Katz, G. and Giesbrecht, E. (2006). Automatic identification of non-compositional multi-word expressions using latent semantic analysis. In *Proceedings of the Workshop on Multiword Expressions: Identifying and Exploiting Underlying Properties*, MWE '06, pages 12–19, Stroudsburg, PA, USA. Association for Computational Linguistics.

Kilgarriff, A., Rychly, P., Smrz, P., and Tugwell, D. (2004). The sketch engine. In *Proceedings of EURALEX*.

Lexical Computing Ltd. (2007). Statistics used in the sketch engine.

McCarthy, D., Keller, B., and Carroll, J. (2003). Detecting a continuum of compositionality in phrasal verbs. In *Proceedings of the ACL 2003 workshop on Multiword expressions: analysis, acquisition and treatment - Volume 18*, MWE '03, pages 73–80, Stroudsburg, PA, USA. Association for Computational Linguistics.

Mitchell, J. and Lapata, M. (2008). Vector-based Models of Semantic Composition. In *Proceedings of ACL-08: HLT*, pages 236–244, Columbus, Ohio. Association for Computational Linguistics.

Murphy, G. L. (2002). *The Big Book of Concepts*. The MIT Press.

Partee, B. (1995). Lexical semantics and compositionality. *L. Gleitman and M. Liberman (eds.) Language, which is Volume 1 of D. Osherson (ed.) An Invitation to Cognitive Science (2nd Edition)*, pages 311–360.

Reisinger, J. and Mooney, R. J. (2010). Multi-prototype vector-space models of word meaning. In *Proceedings of the 11th Annual Conference of the North American Chapter of the Association for Computational Linguistics (NAACL-2010)*, pages 109–117.

Rychlý, P. and Kilgarriff, A. (2007). An efficient algorithm for building a distributional thesaurus (and other sketch engine developments). In *Proceedings of the 45th Annual Meeting of the ACL on Interactive Poster and Demonstration Sessions*, ACL '07, pages 41–44, Stroudsburg, PA, USA. Association for Computational Linguistics.

Sahlgren, M. (2006). *The Word-Space Model: Using distributional analysis to represent syntag-*

matic and paradigmatic relations between words in high-dimensional vector spaces. PhD thesis, Stockholm University.

Schone, P. and Jurafsky, D. (2001). Is knowledge-free induction of multiword unit dictionary headwords a solved problem? In *Proceedings of the Conference on Empirical Methods in Natural Language Processing*, EMNLP '01.

Smith, E. E. and Medin, D. L. (1981). *Categories and concepts / Edward E. Smith and Douglas L. Medin*. Harvard University Press, Cambridge, Mass. :.

Turney, P. D. and Pantel, P. (2010). From frequency to meaning: vector space models of semantics. *J. Artif. Int. Res.*, 37:141–188.

Author Index